THE CAMBRIDGE HYMNAL

THE
CAMBRIDGE
HYMNAL

Vocal Edition

EDITED BY
DAVID HOLBROOK AND
ELIZABETH POSTON

CAMBRIDGE UNIVERSITY PRESS
CAMBRIDGE
LONDON · NEW YORK · MELBOURNE

Published by the Syndics of the Cambridge University Press
The Pitt Building, Trumpington Street, Cambridge CB2 1RP
Bentley House, 200 Euston Road, London NW1 2DB
32 East 57th Street, New York, NY 10022, USA
296 Beaconsfield Parade, Middle Park, Melbourne 3206, Australia

© Cambridge University Press 1976

ISBN 0 521 20398 8

First published 1976

Printed in Great Britain by
Lowe & Brydone (Printers) Ltd, Thetford, Norfolk

CONTENTS

Copyright and Acknowledgements	v
HYMNS	1
CHRISTMAS HYMNS AND CAROLS	118
APPENDIX	177
Index	189

COPYRIGHT AND ACKNOWLEDGEMENTS

The list below covers every edition of the Cambridge Hymnal and specifies every item (words or music) in which rights are controlled by a copyright holder. Sources and other acknowledgements are also indicated in many cases in the body of the book. Items not listed here may be assumed to be out of copyright.

Performing and recording rights are reserved as part of the copyright, and are administered by the Performing Rights Society, the Mechanical Copyright Protection Society and affiliated bodies throughout the world. Application should be made to these societies for licences to perform, etc.

The publishers and editors are grateful to the proprietors listed below for permission to use copyright material.

1. Setting by William Wordsworth © William Wordsworth 1967, all rights controlled by Cambridge University Press

2. Words from the *Yattendon Hymnal*, by permission of the Oxford University Press

4. Harmonization variants with faux-bourdon and descants for festal use by Michael Paget © Michael Paget 1967, all rights controlled by Cambridge University Press

5. Descants by Elizabeth Poston © Elizabeth Poston 1967, all rights controlled by Cambridge University Press

6. Descant by Elizabeth Poston © Elizabeth Poston 1967, all rights controlled by Cambridge University Press

7. Descant by Elizabeth Poston © Elizabeth Poston 1967, all rights controlled by Cambridge University Press

8(i). English words from the *Wells Office Book* by permission of the Principal, the Theological College, Wells

(ii) Accompaniment to COMPLINE HYMN by Elizabeth Poston, © Elizabeth Poston 1967, all rights controlled by Cambridge University Press

(iii) Accompaniment of TE LUCIS ANTE TERMINUM by Elizabeth Poston © Elizabeth Poston 1967, all rights controlled by Cambridge University Press

9. Melody in the bass, three-part harmonization by Elizabeth Poston © Elizabeth Poston 1967, all rights controlled by Cambridge University Press.

10. Descant by Elizabeth Poston © Elizabeth Poston 1967, all rights controlled by Cambridge University Press

12. Descant by Elizabeth Poston © Elizabeth Poston 1967, all rights controlled by Cambridge University Press

15. Harmony revised and descant by Elizabeth Poston © Elizabeth Poston 1967, all rights controlled by Cambridge University Press

16. Harmonization by Elizabeth Poston © Elizabeth Poston 1967, all rights controlled by Cambridge University Press

17. Thomas Campion's melody and setting (*Babylon's Streams*) transcribed and edited by E. H. Fellowes, reproduced from *English Lutenist Song Writers* by permission of the publishers, Stainer and Bell Ltd.

18. Plainchant melody JAM LUCIS, accompaniment by Elizabeth Poston © Elizabeth Poston 1967, all rights controlled by Cambridge University Press

19. Descant by Elizabeth Poston © Elizabeth Poston 1967, all rights controlled by Cambridge University Press

21. Setting by R. Vaughan Williams and adaptation by E. Harold Geer reprinted by permission of Stainer and Bell Ltd. and Yale University Press.

22. Descant and harmony revised by W. R. Pasfield © W. R. Pasfield 1967, all rights controlled by Cambridge University Press

24. Words by T. S. Eliot (from *Murder in the Cathedral*) by permission of Faber and Faber Ltd. London, and Harcourt, Brace, and World Publishing Company, New York. Setting, *Judicium*, by Percy Buck, by permission of Oxford University Press

25. Setting by Gordon Jacob © Gordon Jacob 1967, all rights controlled by Cambridge University Press

26. Descant by Benjamin Britten © 1958 by Hawkes and Son London Ltd., from *Noye's Fludde* by Benjamin Britten, published by Boosey and Hawkes Music Publishers Ltd.

27. Harmonization by Elizabeth Poston © Elizabeth Poston 1967, all rights controlled by Cambridge University Press

29. Descant by Elizabeth Poston © Elizabeth Poston 1967, all rights controlled by Cambridge University Press

30. Setting by Arthur Oldham © Arthur Oldham 1967, all rights controlled by Cambridge University Press

31. Descant by Elizabeth Poston © Elizabeth Poston 1967, all rights controlled by Cambridge University Press

32. Arrangement by Elizabeth Poston © Elizabeth Poston 1967, all rights controlled by Cambridge University Press

34. Harmonization by Benjamin Britten © 1958 by Hawkes and Son London Ltd., from *Noye's Fludde* by Benjamin Britten, published by Boosey and Hawkes Music Publishers Ltd. London

35. Words by Gerard Manley Hopkins, by permission of Oxford University Press. Plainsong melody. Harmonization and accompaniment by Elizabeth Poston © Elizabeth Poston 1967, all rights controlled by Cambridge University Press.

36. Setting by William Wordsworth © William Wordsworth 1967, all rights controlled by Cambridge University Press

37. Descant by Elizabeth Poston © Elizabeth Poston 1967, all rights controlled by Cambridge University Press

38. Descant by Elizabeth Poston © Elizabeth Poston 1967, all rights controlled by Cambridge University Press

39. Harmonization and descant by Elizabeth Poston © Elizabeth Poston 1967, all rights controlled by Cambridge University Press

40. Setting by Lennox Berkeley © Lennox Berkeley 1967, all rights controlled by Cambridge University Press

41. Words by W. H. Auden from *For the Time Being* reproduced by permission of Faber and Faber Ltd., London, and Random House, New York. Setting by Sir Arthur Bliss © Arthur Bliss 1967, all rights controlled by Cambridge University Press

42. Setting by Sir Adrian Beecham © Adrian Beecham 1967, all rights controlled by Cambridge University Press

43. Adaptation of a traditional Irish melody by Havelock Nelson © Havelock Nelson 1967, all rights controlled by Cambridge University Press

44. Setting by John Joubert © John Joubert 1967, all rights controlled by Cambridge University Press

45. Harmonization and descant by Elizabeth Poston © Elizabeth Poston 1967, all rights controlled by Cambridge University Press

46. Descant by Elizabeth Poston © Elizabeth Poston 1967, all rights controlled by Cambridge University Press

47. 'Tallis's Ordinal' arranged with variants for festal use by Elizabeth Poston © Elizabeth Poston 1967, performing and mechanical reproduction rights controlled by Cambridge University Press, all other rights controlled by the composer

49. Arrangement by Elizabeth Poston © Elizabeth Poston 1967, all rights controlled by Cambridge University Press

51. Setting by Gustav Holst, by kind permission of Miss Imogen Holst and the Trustees of the late Gustav Holst

52. Setting by Edmund Rubbra © Alfred Lengnick and Co. Ltd., London, 1967, all rights controlled by Alfred Lengnick

54. Descant by Elizabeth Poston © Elizabeth Poston 1967, all rights controlled by Cambridge University Press

55. Descant by Elizabeth Poston © Elizabeth Poston 1967, all rights controlled by Cambridge University Press

56. Descant by Elizabeth Poston © Elizabeth Poston 1967, all rights controlled by Cambridge University Press

57. Descant by Elizabeth Poston © Elizabeth Poston 1967, all rights controlled by Cambridge University Press

58. Setting by William Mathias © William Mathias 1967, all rights controlled by Cambridge University Press

59. Harmonization and descant by Elizabeth Poston © Elizabeth Poston 1967, all rights controlled by Cambridge University Press

60. Transcribed and adapted by Miss Marylin Wailes, reproduced by permission of Miss Wailes and the publishers, Schott and Co., London

61. Words by Andrew Young by permission of the author, the Rev. Canon Andrew Young.
62. The setting 'Wiveton' by Lennox Berkeley © Lennox Berkeley 1967; the setting 'Erwin' by Herbert Howells © Herbert Howells 1967, all rights in both hymns are controlled by Cambridge University Press

63. Setting by Sir Adrian Beecham © Adrian Beecham 1967, all rights controlled by Cambridge University Press

64. Harmonization and descant by Elizabeth Poston © Elizabeth Poston 1967, all rights controlled by Cambridge University Press

66. Setting by Edric Cundell © Estate of Edric Cundell 1967, descant by Elizabeth Poston © Elizabeth Poston 1967, all rights in both controlled by Cambridge University Press

67. Descant by Elizabeth Poston © Elizabeth Poston 1967, all rights controlled by Cambridge University Press

68. Harmonization by Elizabeth Poston © Elizabeth Poston 1967, all rights controlled by Cambridge University Press

69. Words, cento Percy Dearmer, by permission of the copyright holders, Oxford University Press. Harmonization and descant by Elizabeth Poston © Elizabeth Poston 1967, all rights controlled by Cambridge University Press

71. Inner parts of 'Jouissance' added by Elizabeth Poston © Elizabeth Poston 1967, all rights controlled by Cambridge University Press
72. Descant by Elizabeth Poston © Elizabeth Poston 1967, all rights controlled by Cambridge University Press
73. Descant by Elizabeth Poston © Elizabeth Poston 1967, all rights controlled by Cambridge University Press
75. Arranged by Elizabeth Poston from the transcription by Peter Warlock. Reproduced by permission of the copyright holders, Oxford University Press
76. Setting by Arthur Oldham © Arthur Oldham 1967, all rights controlled by Cambridge University Press
77. Realisation by David Willcocks of the figured bass by Henry Purcell © David Willcocks 1967, all rights controlled by Cambridge University Press.
79. Descant and faux-bourdon by John Gardner © John Gardner 1967, all rights controlled by Cambridge University Press
80. Festal version with trumpets by Elizabeth Poston © Elizabeth Poston 1967, all rights controlled by Cambridge University Press
81. Descant by Elizabeth Poston © Elizabeth Poston 1967, all rights controlled by Cambridge University Press
82. Harmony revised by Elizabeth Poston © Elizabeth Poston 1967, all rights controlled by Cambridge University Press
83. Setting by Arthur Oldham © Arthur Oldham 1967, all rights controlled by Cambridge University Press
84. Words (paraphrase by Robert Bridges) from the *Yattendon Hymnal*, by permission of the publishers, Oxford University Press
85. Descant by Elizabeth Poston © Elizabeth Poston 1967, all rights controlled by Cambridge University Press
86. Harmonization by Elizabeth Poston © Elizabeth Poston 1967, all rights controlled by Cambridge University Press
87. Descant by Elizabeth Poston © Elizabeth Poston 1967, all rights controlled by Cambridge University Press
88. Setting by Alan Ridout © Alan Ridout 1967, all rights controlled by Cambridge University Press
89. Setting by Edward Elgar reproduced by permission of Novello and Co., Mrs Elgar Blake and the Elgar Trustees. All rights controlled by the Elgar Trust. Descant by Elizabeth Poston © Elizabeth Poston 1967, all rights controlled by the Elgar Trust
90. Descant by Elizabeth Poston © Elizabeth Poston 1967, all rights controlled by Cambridge University Press
91. Descant by Elizabeth Poston © Elizabeth Poston 1967, all rights controlled by Cambridge University Press
92. Words and music by Thomas Campion, transcribed and edited by E. H. Fellowes and published by Stainer and Bell Ltd. in *English Lutenist Song Writers*, by permission of the publishers. Descant by Elizabeth Poston © Elizabeth Poston 1967, all rights controlled by Cambridge University Press
94. Harmonization by Elizabeth Poston © Elizabeth Poston 1967, all rights controlled by Cambridge University Press
95. Setting by Wilfrid Mellers © Wilfrid Mellers 1967, all rights controlled by Cambridge University Press

96. Setting by Sir Arthur Bliss © Arthur Bliss 1967, all rights controlled by Cambridge University Press

97. Setting by William Wordsworth © William Wordsworth 1967, all rights controlled by Cambridge University Press

98. Setting by William Wordsworth © William Wordsworth 1967, all rights controlled by Cambridge University Press

99. Descant by Elizabeth Poston © Elizabeth Poston 1967, all rights controlled by Cambridge University Press

101. Setting and descant by John Gardner © John Gardner 1967, all rights controlled by Cambridge University Press

102. Arrangement by Elizabeth Poston © Elizabeth Poston 1967, all rights controlled by Cambridge University Press

103. Harmonization and descant by Elizabeth Poston © Elizabeth Poston 1967, all rights controlled by Cambridge University Press

104. Harmonization and descant by Elizabeth Poston © Elizabeth Poston 1967, all rights controlled by Cambridge University Press

105. English words from the *Wells Office Book*, by permission of the Principal, The Theological College, Wells
Accompaniment, TE LUCIS, of plainchant melody, by Elizabeth Poston © Elizabeth Poston 1967, all rights controlled by Cambridge University Press. Accompaniment, ST. AMBROSE, of second plainchant melody, by Elizabeth Poston © Elizabeth Poston 1967, all rights controlled by Cambridge University Press

106. Setting by Edmund Rubbra reproduced by permission of Alfred Lengnick & Co. Ltd.

107. Arrangement by Maurice Jacobson © Maurice Jacobson 1967, all rights controlled by Cambridge University Press

108. Arrangement by Elizabeth Poston © Elizabeth Poston 1967, all rights controlled by Cambridge University Press

109. Harmonization and descant by Elizabeth Poston © Elizabeth Poston 1967, all rights controlled by Cambridge University Press

110. Words by Sir Thomas Browne slightly altered by the editors, *Cambridge Hymnal*. Setting by Ralph Vaughan Williams reprinted from *Songs of Praise* by permission of the publishers, Oxford University Press

111. Setting by Elizabeth Poston © Elizabeth Poston 1967, performing and mechanical reproduction rights controlled by Cambridge University Press; other rights controlled by the composer

112. Descant by Elizabeth Poston © Elizabeth Poston 1967, all rights controlled by Cambridge University Press

113. Setting by John Gardner © John Gardner 1967, all rights controlled by Cambridge University Press

114. Hymn Tune prelude by Elizabeth Poston © Elizabeth Poston 1967, all rights controlled by Cambridge University Press

115. Setting by Elizabeth Poston © Elizabeth Poston 1967, all rights controlled by Cambridge University Press

117. Arrangement by Aaron Copland © Aaron Copland 1950, by permission of the composer and the publishers, Boosey and Hawkes Music Publishers Ltd.

118. Setting by John Joubert © John Joubert 1967, all rights controlled by Cambridge University Press
119. Arrangement by Elizabeth Poston © Elizabeth Poston 1967; all rights controlled by Cambridge University Press
120. Accompaniment of VENI CREATOR by Anthony Milner © Anthony Milner 1967, all rights controlled by Cambridge University Press
121. Metrical version of VENI CREATOR by Anthony Milner © Anthony Milner 1967, all rights controlled by Cambridge University Press
122. Melody (*Babylon's Streams*) and setting transcribed and edited by E. H. Fellowes in *English Lutenist Song Writers*, reproduced by permission of the publishers, Stainer and Bell Ltd.
123. Harmonization by Elizabeth Poston © Elizabeth Poston 1967, all rights controlled by Cambridge University Press
125. Descant by Elizabeth Poston © Elizabeth Poston 1967; all rights controlled by Cambridge University Press
126. Accompaniment by Elizabeth Poston © Elizabeth Poston 1967, all rights controlled by Cambridge University Press
127. Words and music transcribed and edited by E. H. Fellowes in *English Lutenist Song Writers*, reproduced by permission of the publishers, Stainer and Bell Ltd.
128. Setting MONK'S GATE by Ralph Vaughan Williams, by permission of the publishers, Oxford University Press
129. Words and music transcribed and edited by E. H. Fellowes in *English Lutenist Song Writers*, reproduced by permission of the publishers, Stainer and Bell Ltd. Descant by Elizabeth Poston © Elizabeth Poston 1967, all rights controlled by Cambridge University Press
130. Realisation by Elizabeth Poston © Elizabeth Poston 1967, all rights controlled by Cambridge University Press
131. Setting by Havelock Nelson © Havelock Nelson 1967, all rights controlled by Cambridge University Press
132. Arrangement by Elizabeth Poston © Elizabeth Poston 1967; all rights controlled by Cambridge University Press
134. Arrangement by Elizabeth Poston © Elizabeth Poston 1967, all rights controlled by Cambridge University Press
135. Arrangement by Elizabeth Poston © Elizabeth Poston 1967, all rights controlled by Cambridge University Press
136. Descant by John Tooze © Cambridge University Press
137. Revision and descant by Elizabeth Poston © Elizabeth Poston 1967, all rights controlled by Cambridge University Press
138. Descant and harmonization by W. R. Pasfield © W. R. Pasfield 1967, all rights controlled by Cambridge University Press
139. Prelude and harmonization by Elizabeth Poston © Elizabeth Poston 1967, all rights controlled by Cambridge University Press
140. Setting by Norman Fulton © Norman Fulton 1967, all rights controlled by Cambridge University Press
141. Arrangement by Elizabeth Poston © Elizabeth Poston 1967; performing and mechanical reproduction rights controlled by Cambridge University Press, other rights controlled by the composer
142. Setting by Norman Fulton, © Norman Fulton 1967, all rights controlled by Cambridge University Press

143. Arrangement by Elizabeth Poston © Elizabeth Poston 1967; performing and mechanical reproduction rights controlled by Cambridge University Press, other rights controlled by the composer

144. Traditional words and melody arranged by Elizabeth Poston © Elizabeth Poston 1967; performing and mechanical reproduction rights controlled by Cambridge University Press, and other rights controlled by the composer

145. Traditional words and melody collected by Ralph Vaughan Williams, published in his arrangement in *Eight Traditional Carols*, and reproduced by permission of the publishers, Stainer and Bell Ltd. New arrangement by Nicholas Maw first published in this Hymnal © Nicholas Maw 1967, all rights controlled by Cambridge University Press

146. Descant by Elizabeth Poston © Elizabeth Poston 1967, all rights controlled by Cambridge University Press

147. Arrangement by Michael Paget © Michael Paget 1967, all rights controlled by Cambridge University Press

148. Arrangement by Elizabeth Poston © Elizabeth Poston 1967; performing and mechanical reproduction rights controlled by Cambridge University Press, other rights controlled by composer

149. W. H. Cummings's adaptation of Mendelssohn's original music is reproduced by kind permission of the original publishers, Novello and Co. Ltd.

150. Folk carol melody collected by Cecil Sharp, reproduced by permission of Novello and Co. Ltd.; setting by Benjamin Britten (S.A.T.B.) copyright 1957 by Boosey and Hawkes Music Publishers Ltd.

151. Setting by Stanley Taylor © Stanley Taylor 1967, all rights controlled by Cambridge University Press

152. Setting by Lennox Berkeley © Lennox Berkeley 1967, all rights controlled by Cambridge University Press

153. Setting by Christopher Morris © Christopher Morris 1967, all rights controlled by Cambridge University Press

154. Setting by Gustav Holst, © Miss Imogen Holst and the Trustees of the late Gustav Holst, by kind permission of the Trustees

155. Arrangement by Elizabeth Poston © Elizabeth Poston 1967; performing and mechanical reproduction rights controlled by Cambridge University Press, all other rights controlled by the composer

156. Setting by Peter Warlock, copyright in U.S.A. and all countries 1928 by the Oxford University Press, London, reproduced by permission of the publishers

157. Setting by William Mathias © William Mathias 1967, all rights controlled by Cambridge University Press

158. Traditional Virginian words and melody © John Jacob Niles collected by John Jacob Niles, reproduced by permission of the publishers, G. Schirmer Inc. Arrangement by Elizabeth Poston © Elizabeth Poston 1967, all rights controlled by Cambridge University Press

159. Words from *Collected Poems* by Andrew Young, © Rupert Hart Davis 1960, by permission of the publisher. Setting by Elizabeth Poston © Elizabeth Poston 1967, all rights controlled by Cambridge University Press

160. Setting by Alan Ridout © Alan Ridout 1967, all rights controlled by Cambridge University Press

161. Setting by Gustav Holst, reproduced by permission of the publishers, J. Curwen & Sons Ltd.

162. Words from a MS. in the Library of Trinity College, Cambridge, by permission of the Master and Fellows. Setting by Elizabeth Maconchy © Elizabeth Maconchy 1967, all rights controlled by Cambridge University Press

163. Scottish traditional melody arranged by Elizabeth Poston © Elizabeth Poston 1967; performing and mechanical reproduction rights controlled by Cambridge University Press, all other rights controlled by the composer

164. Descant by Elizabeth Poston © Elizabeth Poston 1967, all rights controlled by Cambridge University Press

165. Traditional Sussex carol collected and arranged by R. Vaughan Williams in *Eight Traditional Carols* by permission of the publishers, Stainer and Bell Ltd. Adaptation by E. Harold Geer reproduced by permission of Yale University Press from *Hymnal for Schools and Colleges*

166. Harmonized by Anthony Milner © Anthony Milner 1967, all rights controlled by Cambridge University Press

167. Kentucky folk carol collected by John Jacob Niles, reproduced by permission of the publishers, G. Schirmer Inc., New York (Chappell and Co. Ltd., London). Arrangement by Elizabeth Poston © Elizabeth Poston 1967, all rights controlled by Cambridge University Press

168. Setting by Stanley Taylor © 1967 J. Curwen and Sons Ltd., 29 Maiden Lane, London, W.C.2

169. Setting by Imogen Holst © Imogen Holst 1967, all rights controlled by Cambridge University Press

170. Setting by Ralph Vaughan Williams (from *Hodie*) © Oxford University Press, by permission of the publishers

171. Words and melody reprinted from the Edric Connor Collection of West Indian Spirituals and Folk Tunes, by permission of Boosey and Hawkes Music Publishers Ltd. Arrangement by Elizabeth Poston © Elizabeth Poston 1967

172. Words reproduced by permission of the Master and Fellows of Trinity
173. College, Cambridge. Music originally transcribed and edited by John Stevens in *Musica Britannica* Vol. IV; © the Royal Musical Association (agents Stainer and Bell Ltd.) Simplified version (173) edited by John Stevens, also by permission of Stainer and Bell Ltd.

174. Arrangement by Elizabeth Poston © Elizabeth Poston 1967; performing and mechanical reproduction rights controlled by Cambridge University Press, all other rights controlled by the composer

175. Arrangement by Elizabeth Poston © Elizabeth Poston 1967; performing
176. and mechanical reproduction rights controlled by Cambridge University Press, all other rights controlled by the composer

177. Arrangement by Elizabeth Poston © Elizabeth Poston 1967, all rights controlled by Cambridge University Press

178. Melody in the tenor harmonization by Elizabeth Poston © Elizabeth Poston 1967; performing and mechanical rights controlled by Cambridge University Press, all other rights controlled by the composer

179. Setting by Benjamin Britten © 1963 by Boosey and Co. Ltd.; reprinted by permission of Boosey and Hawkes Music Publishers Ltd.

180. Setting by Elizabeth Maconchy © Elizabeth Maconchy 1967, all rights controlled by Cambridge University Press

181. Setting by John Gardner © John Gardner 1967, all rights controlled by Cambridge University Press

182. From a Yoruba hymn by the Rev. Ola Olude, by permission of the composer; arrangement by Fela Sowande © Fela Sowande 1967, all rights controlled by Cambridge University Press

183. Setting by Igor Stravinsky, adapted by Elizabeth Poston, by permission, printed by permission of the publishers, J. and W. Chester Ltd.

184. Setting by Guy Oldham © Guy Oldham 1967, all rights controlled by Cambridge University Press

186. Arrangement by Elizabeth Poston © Elizabeth Poston 1967; performing and mechanical reproduction rights controlled by Cambridge University Press, all other rights controlled by the composer

187. Setting by John Gardner © John Gardner 1967, all rights controlled by Cambridge University Press

188. Setting by John Gardner © John Gardner 1967, all rights controlled by Cambridge University Press

190, Words by W. H. Auden, from his *For the Time Being*, printed by permission
191. of the publishers, Faber and Faber Ltd., London, and Random House, New York. Setting by Norman Fulton © Norman Fulton 1967, all rights controlled by Cambridge University Press

192. Words by Gerard Manley Hopkins by permission of the publishers, Oxford University Press. Setting by William Wordsworth © William Wordsworth 1967, all rights controlled by Cambridge University Press

193 Words by Edna St Vincent Millay © 1912 by Edna St Vincent Millay from *Renascence* in *Renascence and Other Poems*, published by Harper Brothers, by permission of the publishers. Setting by Elizabeth Poston © Elizabeth Poston 1967, all rights controlled by Cambridge University Press

HYMNS

1 Ah, my dear Lord! what couldst thou spy
  In this impure, rebellious clay,
 That made thee thus resolve to die
  For those that kill thee every day?

2 O what strange wonders could thee move
  To slight thy precious blood, and breath!
 Sure it was Love, my Lord; for Love
  Is only stronger far than death.

Henry Vaughan, 1622–95

2

HERZLIEBSTER JESU

Melody by J. Crüger, 1598–1662

1. Ah, holy Jesu, how hast thou offended,
   That man to judge thee hath in hate pretended?
   By foes derided, by thine own rejected,
   O most afflicted.

2. Who was the guilty? Who brought this upon thee?
   Alas, my treason, Jesu, hath undone thee.
   'Twas I, Lord Jesu, I it was denied thee,
   I crucified thee.

3. For me, kind Jesu, was thy incarnation,
   Thy mortal sorrow, and thy life's oblation;
   Thy death of sorrow, and thy bitter passion,
   For my salvation.

Johann Heerman, 1585–1647
Paraphrased by Robert Bridges, 1844–1930 (abridged by the Editors)
By permission of the Yattendon Hymnal

J. S. Bach (1685–1750) in the *Passion according to St. Matthew*

3

ST. THEODULPH

Melody by Melchior Teschner, *c.* 1613

1 All glory, laud, and honour
  To thee, Redeemer, King,
To whom the lips of children
  Made sweet hosannas ring.
Thou art the King of Israel,
  Thou David's royal Son,
Who in the Lord's name comest,
  The King and blessèd one.

2 The company of angels
  Are praising thee on high,
And mortal men and all things
  Created make reply.
The people of the Hebrews
  With palms before thee went;
Our praise and prayer and anthems
  Before thee we present.

3 To thee before thy Passion
    They sang their hymns of praise;
  To thee now high exalted
    Our melody we raise.
  Thou didst accept their praises;
    Accept the prayers we bring
  Who in all good delightest,
    Thou good and gracious King.

4 All glory, laud, and honour
    To thee, Redeemer, King,
  To whom the lips of children
    Made sweet hosannas ring.

St. Theodulph of Orleans, d. 821
Translated by J. M. Neale, 1818–66

ALTERNATIVE VERSION

Adapted by J. S. Bach (1685–1750)

ST. THEODULPH (VALET WILL ICH DIR GEBEN)

4

OLD HUNDREDTH
Slow and dignified Melody from *Genevan Psalter* (L. Bourgeois, 1550)

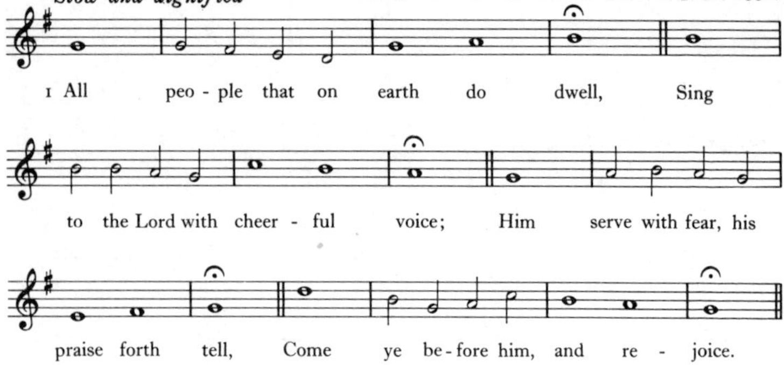

1 All people that on earth do dwell, Sing to the Lord with cheer-ful voice; Him serve with fear, his praise forth tell, Come ye be-fore him, and re - joice.

VERSE 5
Vocal or instrumental descant (optional trumpet) Michael Paget, 1936–

5 To Fa-ther, Son and Ho-ly Ghost, The God whom heav'n and earth a - dore, From men and from the an - gel host __ Be praise and glo-ry e - ver - more.

5 To Fa-ther, Son and Ho-ly Ghost, The God whom heav'n and earth a - dore, From men and from the an - gel host Be praise and glo-ry e - ver - more.

1 All people that on earth do dwell,
　Sing to the Lord with cheerful voice;
Him serve with fear, his praise forth tell,
　Come ye before him, and rejoice.

2 The Lord, ye know, is God indeed,
　Without our aid he did us make;
We are his folk, he doth us feed,
　And for his sheep he doth us take.

3 O enter then his gates with praise,
　Approach with joy his courts unto;
Praise, laud, and bless his name always,
　For it is seemly so to do.

4 For why, the Lord our God is good:
　His mercy is for ever sure;
His truth at all times firmly stood,
　And shall from age to age endure.

5 To Father, Son and Holy Ghost,
　The God whom heav'n and earth adore,
From men and from the angel-host
　Be praise and glory evermore.

W. Kethe, Day's Psalter 1560–1

5

SONG 6,7

ORLANDO GIBBONS, 1583–1625
Descant, E. P.

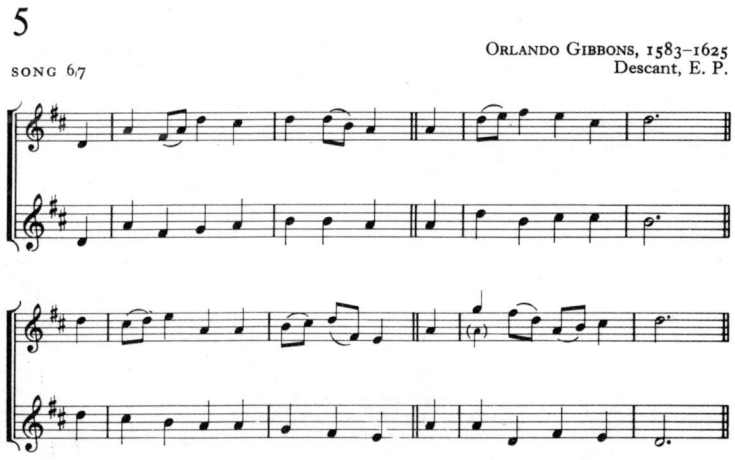

1 And now another day is gone,
　I'll sing my Maker's praise,
My comforts every hour make known,
　His providence and grace.

2 I lay my body down to sleep;
　May angels guard my head,
And through the hours of darkness keep
　Their watch around my bed.

3 With cheerful heart I close my eyes,
　Since thou wilt not remove;
And in the morning let me rise
　Rejoicing in thy love.

Isaac Watts, 1674–1748

6

MARTYRDOM

R. A. Smith's *Sacred Music*, 1825
Descant, E. P.

1 As pants the hart for cooling streams
  When heated in the chase,
 So longs my soul, O God, for thee,
  And thy refreshing grace.

2 For thee, my God, the living God,
  My thirsty soul doth pine:
 O when shall I behold thy face,
  Thou Majesty divine?

3 Why restless, why cast down, my soul?
  Hope still, and thou shalt sing
 The praise of him who is thy God,
  Thy health's eternal spring.

4 To Father, Son, and Holy Ghost,
  The God whom we adore,
 Be glory, as it was, is now,
  And shall be evermore.

Nahum Tate (1652–1715) and Nicholas Brady (1659–1726), 'New Version,' 1696
From Psalm 42

7

WAREHAM

W. Knapp, 1698–1768
Descant, E. P.

1. Be with me, Lord, where'er I go;
   Teach me what thou wouldst have me do;
   Suggest whate'er I think or say;
   Direct me in thy narrow way.

2. Prevent me, lest I harbour pride,
   Lest I in my own strength confide;
   Show me my weakness, let me see
   I have my power, my all from thee.

3. Assist and teach me how to pray;
   Incline my nature to obey;
   What thou abhorrest let me flee,
   And only love what pleases thee.

J. Cennick, 1718–55 (altered)

8

COMPLINE HYMN
ST. AMBROSE

Plainchant, from La Feillée,
Méthode du plain-chant, 1782

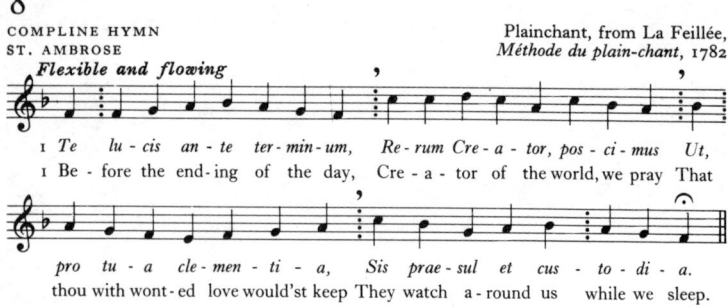

1 Te lucis ante terminum, Rerum Creator, poscimus Ut, pro tua clementia, Sis praesul et custodia.

1 Before the ending of the day, Creator of the world, we pray That thou with wonted love would'st keep Thy watch around us while we sleep.

TE LUCIS ANTE TERMINUM

Melody, *Andernach Gesangbuch*, 1608

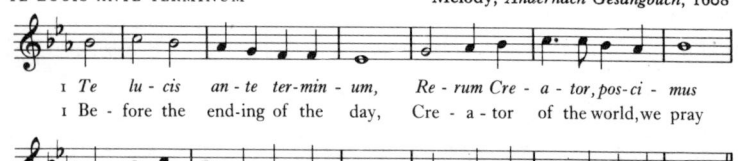

1. Te lucis ante terminum,
   Rerum Creator, poscimus
   Ut, pro tua clementia,
   Sis praesul et custodia.

2. Praesta, Pater piissime,
   Patrique compar unice,
   Cum Spiritu Paraclito
   Regnans per omne saeculum.

Before 8th century

1. Before the ending of the day,
   Creator of the world, we pray
   That thou with wonted love would'st keep
   Thy watch around us while we sleep.

2. Almighty Father, hear our cry,
   Through Jesus Christ, our Lord most high,
   Who, with the Holy Ghost and thee,
   Doth live and reign eternally.

Version from Wells Office Book, by permission
(Both versions abbreviated by the Editors)

9

FRANCONIA

W. H. HAVERGAL, 1793–1870
(founded on a melody by J. B. König, 1691–1758)

1 Blest are the pure in heart,
  For they shall see our God;
  The secret of the Lord is theirs,
  Their soul is Christ's abode.

2 The Lord, who left the heavens
  Our life and peace to bring,
  To dwell in lowliness with men,
  Their pattern and their King.

3 Still to the lowly soul
  He doth himself impart,
  And for his dwelling and his throne
  Chooseth the pure in heart.

4 Lord, we thy presence seek;
  May ours this blessing be:
  Give us a pure and lowly heart,
  A temple meet for thee.

J. Keble, 1792–1866, and others

10

TIVERTON

— GRIGG, in *John Rippon's Selection of Psalms and Hymn Tunes*, c. 1790
Descant, E. P.

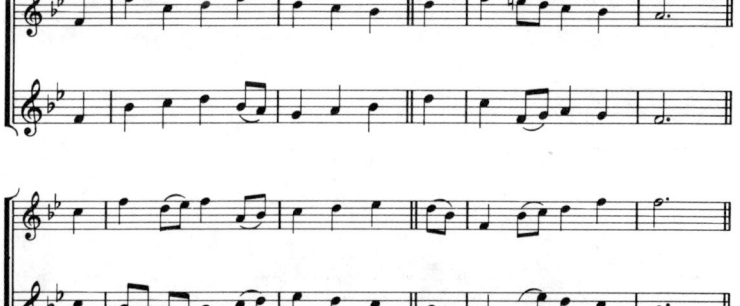

1 Blest be the day that I began
  A pilgrim for to be;
  And blessèd also be that man
  That thereto movèd me.

2 'Tis true, 'twas long ere I began
  To seek to live for ever;
  But now I run fast as I can;
  'Tis better late than never.

3 Some of the ditch shy are, yet can
  Lie tumbling in the mire;
  Some, though they shun the frying pan,
  Do leap into the fire.

4 What danger is the pilgrim in,
  How many are his foes!
  How many ways there are to sin
  No living mortal knows.

5 The Lord is only my support
  And he that doth me feed;
  How can I then want anything
  Whereof I stand in need?

6 Our tears to joy, our fears to faith,
  Are turnèd as we see,
  That our beginning, as one saith,
  Shows what our end will be.

John Bunyan, 1628–88, from 'The Pilgrim's Progress'

11

RENDEZ À DIEU

Melody composed or adapted by L. Bourgeois
in the *Genevan Psalter*, 1543

Bread of the world in mercy broken,
  Wine of the soul, in mercy shed,
By whom the words of life were spoken,
  And in whose death our sins are dead:
Look on the heart by sorrow broken,
  Look on the tears by sinners shed,
And be thy feast to us the token
  That by thy grace our souls are fed.

Reginald Heber, 1783–1826

12

TUNBRIDGE

Jeremiah Clark, 1670–1707
Descant, E. P.

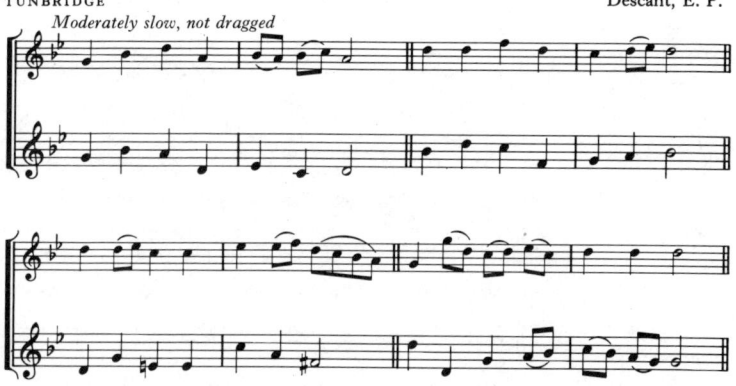

1. Can I see another's woe,
   And not be in sorrow too?
   Can I see another's grief,
   And not seek for kind relief?

2. Can I see a falling tear,
   And not feel my sorrow's share?
   Can a father see his child
   Weep, nor be with sorrow filled?

3. Can a mother sit and hear
   An infant groan an infant fear?
   No, No! never can it be!
   Never, never can it be!

4. And can he who smiles on all
   Hear the wren with sorrows small,
   Hear the small bird's grief and care,
   Hear the woes that infants bear,

5. And not sit beside the nest,
   Pouring pity in their breast;
   And not sit the cradle near,
   Weeping tear on infant's tear;

6. And not sit both night and day
   Wiping all our tears away?
   O, no! never can it be!
   Never, never can it be!

7. He doth give his joy to all;
   He becomes an infant small,
   He becomes a man of woe;
   He doth feel the sorrow too.

8. Think not thou canst sigh a sigh,
   And thy maker is not by;
   Think not thou canst weep a tear,
   And thy maker is not near.

9. O! he gives to us his joy
   That our grief he may destroy;
   Till our grief is fled and gone,
   He doth sit by us and moan.

William Blake, 1757–1827

13

CAST THY BURDEN

Melody from *Meiningen Gesangbuch*, 1693
Adapted by Felix Mendelssohn-Bartholdy, 1809–47

Cast thy burden upon the Lord,
And he shall sustain thee.
He never will suffer the righteous to fall:
He is at thy right hand.
Thy mercy, Lord, is great;
And far above the heav'ns.
Let none be made ashamèd,
That wait upon thee.

? *William Bartholomew*, 1793–1867

* adapted from:

14

WALSALL

From *A Choice Collection of Psalm Tunes*,
W. ANCHORS, *c.* 1721

1 Come Holy Ghost, thine influence shed,
　　And realize the sign;
　Thy life infuse into the bread,
　　Thy power into the wine.

2 Effectual let the tokens prove
　　And made, by heavenly art,
　Fit channels to convey thy love
　　To every faithful heart.

Charles Wesley, 1707–88

15

RATISBON

WERNER, *Choralbuch,* 1815
Descant, E.P.

1 Christ, whose glory fills the skies,
　　Christ, the true, the only light,
　Sun of righteousness, arise,
　　Triumph o'er the shades of night:
　Dayspring from on high, be near;
　Daystar, in my heart appear.

2 Dark and cheerless is the morn
　　Unaccompanied by thee;
　Joyless is the day's return,
　　Till thy mercy's beams I see;
　Till they inward light impart,
　Glad my eyes, and warm my heart.

3 Visit then this soul of mine,
　　Pierce the gloom of sin and grief;
　Fill me, Radiancy divine,
　　Scatter all my unbelief;
　More and more thyself display,
　Shining to the perfect day.

Charles Wesley, 1707–88

16

JOUISSANCE — Melody by PIERRE BONNET, 1638–1708

1 Christ, whose glory fills the skies,
  Christ, the true, the only light,
Sun of righteousness, arise,
  Triumph o'er the shades of night:
Dayspring from on high, be near;
Daystar, in my heart appear.

2 Dark and cheerless is the morn
  Unaccompanied by thee;
Joyless is the day's return,
  Till thy mercy's beams I see;
Till they inward light impart,
Glad my eyes, and warm my heart.

3 Visit then this soul of mine,
  Pierce the gloom of sin and grief;
Fill me, Radiancy divine,
  Scatter all my unbelief;
More and more thyself display,
Shining to the perfect day.

Charles Wesley, 1707–88

17

BABYLON'S STREAMS — THOMAS CAMPION, 1575–1619
Transcribed and edited by E. H. Fellowes, 1870–1951

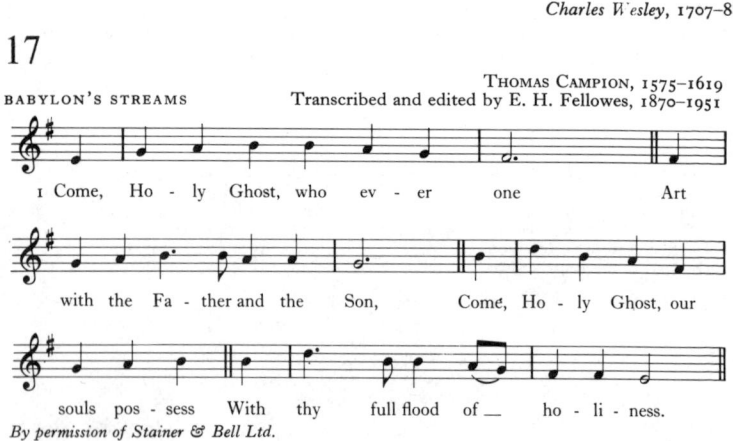

By permission of Stainer & Bell Ltd.

1. Come, Holy Ghost, who ever one
   Art with the Father and the Son,
   Come, Holy Ghost, our souls possess
   With thy full flood of holiness.

2. In will and deed, in heart and tongue,
   With all thy powers, thy praise be sung;
   And love light up our mortal frame
   Till others catch the living flame.

3. Almighty Father, hear our cry
   Through Jesus Christ our Lord most high,
   Who with the Holy Ghost and thee
   Both live and reign eternally.

St. Ambrose, 340–97
Translated by J. H. Newman, 1801–90

18

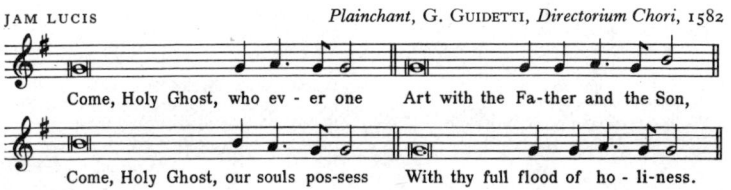

JAM LUCIS — *Plainchant, G. Guidetti, Directorium Chori, 1582*

Come, Holy Ghost, who ev-er one Art with the Fa-ther and the Son,
Come, Holy Ghost, our souls pos-sess With thy full flood of ho-li-ness.

19

NATIVITY

H. Lahee, 1826–1912
Descant, E. P.

1. Come, let us join our cheerful songs
   With angels round the throne;
   Ten thousand thousand are their tongues,
   But all their joys are one.

2. 'Worthy the Lamb that died,' they cry,
   'To be exalted thus!'
   'Worthy the Lamb,' our lips reply,
   'For he was slain for us.'

3. Jesus is worthy to receive
   Honour and power divine;
   And blessings more than we can give
   Be, Lord, for ever thine.

4. Let all creation join in one
   To bless the sacred name
   Of him that sits upon the throne,
   And to adore the Lamb.

Isaac Watts, 1674–1748
Based on Revelation V, 11–13

20

SONG 13 — ORLANDO GIBBONS, 1583–1625

In moderate time

1 Come, my soul, thy suit prepare:
Jesus loves to answer prayer;
He himself has bid thee pray,
Therefore will not say thee nay.

2 Thou art coming to a king,
Large petitions with thee bring;
For his grace and power are such
None can ever ask too much.

3 Show me what I have to do;
Every hour my strength renew;
Let me live a life of faith,
Let me die thy people's death.

4 While I am a pilgrim here
Let thy love my spirit cheer;
Be my guide, my guard, my friend;
Lead me to my journey's end.

J. Newton, 1725–1807

21

THE CALL

R. VAUGHAN WILLIAMS, 1872–1958 (in *Five Mystical Songs*)
Adapted by E. Harold Geer in *Yale Hymnal for Colleges and Schools*

Moderately slow
UNISON

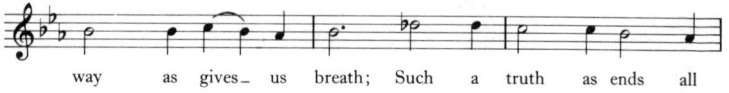

By permission of Stainer & Bell Ltd.

THE CALL

1 Come, my way, my truth, my life:
Such a way as gives us breath;
Such a truth as ends all strife;
Such a life as killeth death.

2 Come, my light, my feast, my strength:
Such a light as shows a feast;
Such a feast as mends in length;
Such a strength as makes his guest.

3 Come, my joy, my love, my heart:
Such a joy as none can move;
Such a love as none can part;
Such a heart as joys in love.

George Herbert, 1593–1633

ST. GEORGE

G. J. ELVEY, 1816–93
Descant by W.R. PASFIELD, 1909–
Commissioned for *The Cambridge Hymnal*

1 Come, O come in pious lays
  Sound we God-Almighty's praise.
  Hither bring, in one consent,
  Heart and voice and instrument.
  Strike the viol, touch the lute
  Let not tongue nor string be mute:
    Nor a creature dumb be found
    That hath either voice or sound.

2 Lowly pipe, ye worms that creep
  On the earth, or in the deep;
  Loud-aloft your voices strain,
  Beasts, and monsters of the main;
  Birds, your warbling treble sing,
  Clouds, your peals of thunder ring.
    Sun and moon, exalted higher
    And bright stars, augment this choir.

3 Come, ye sons of human race,
  In this chorus take a place;
  And, amid the mortal-throng
  Be you masters of the song.
  Let in praise of God the sound
  Run a never-ending round,
    That our song of praise may be
    Everlasting, as is He.

4 From earth's vast and hollow womb
  Music's deepest bass may come;
  To this consort, when we sing,
  Whistling winds, your descants bring.
  That our song may overclimb
  All the bounds of space and time.
    And ascend from sphere to sphere
    To the great Almighty's ear.

5 So, from heaven, on earth, he shall
  Let his gracious blessings fall,
  And this huge wide orb, we see,
  Shall one choir, one temple be,
  Where, in such a praise-full tone,
  We will sing what he hath done.
    Then, O come, in pious lays
    Sound we God-Almighty's praise.

George Wither, 1588–1667

23

NUN LASST UNS GOTT

Melody by NICOLAUS SELNECKER, 1528–92
Version of J.S. BACH, 1685–1750

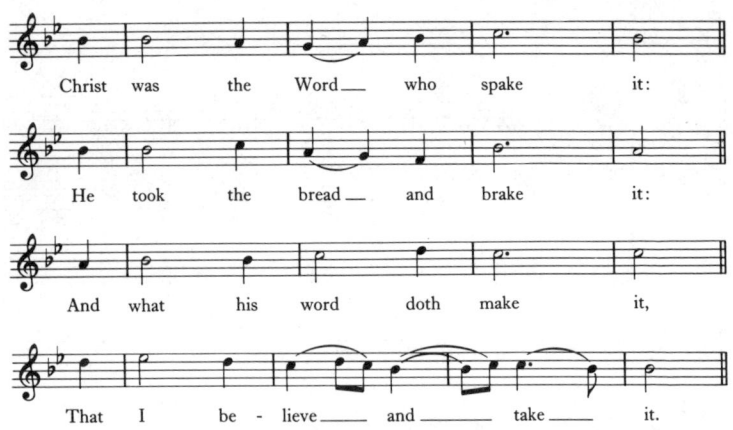

Christ was the Word who spake it:
He took the bread and brake it:
And what his word doth make it,
That I believe and take it.

16th century, sometimes attributed to Queen Elizabeth I

24

JUDICIUM

P. C. BUCK, 1871–1947

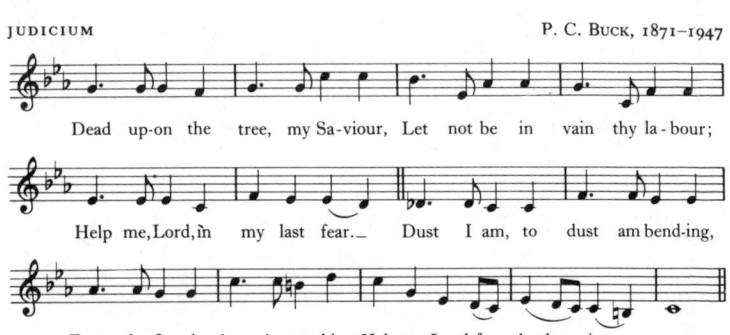

By permission, Oxford University Press, from the Clarendon Hymn Book

Dead upon the tree, my Saviour,
Let not be in vain thy labour;
Help me, Lord, in my last fear.

Dust I am, to dust am bending,
From the final doom impending
Help me, Lord, for death is near.

T. S. Eliot, 1888–1965, from Murder in the Cathedral

25

GORDON JACOB, 1895–
Commissioned for *The Cambridge Hymnal*

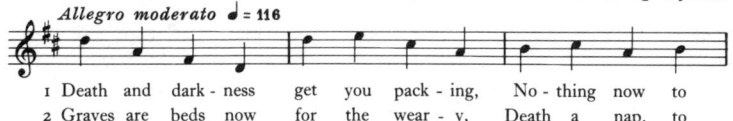
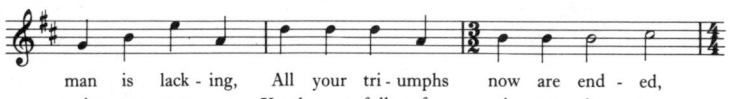

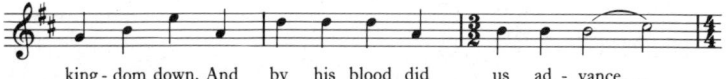

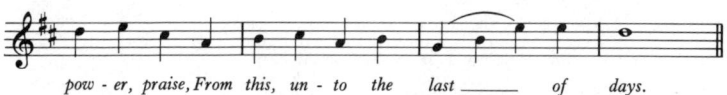

1 Death and darkness get you packing,
Nothing now to man is lacking,
All your triumphs now are ended,
And what Adam marr'd is mended.

2 Graves are beds now for the weary,
Death a nap, to wake more merry;
Youth now, full of pious duty,
Seeks in thee for perfect beauty.

3 Then unto him who thus hath thrown
Ev'n to contempt thy kingdom down,
And by his blood did us advance
Unto his own inheritance,
To him be glory, power, praise,
From this, unto the last of days.

Henry Vaughan, 1622–95

26

MELITA

J. B. Dykes, 1823–76
Descant, Benjamin Britten, 1913–

Copyright 1958 by Hawkes & Son (London) Ltd.

1 Eternal Father, strong to save,
Whose arm hath bound the restless wave,
Who bid'st the mighty ocean deep
Its own appointed limits keep;
  O hear us when we cry to thee
  For all in peril on the sea.

2 O Christ, whose voice the waters heard
And hushed their raging at thy word,
Who walkedst on the foaming deep,
And calm amid the storm didst sleep;
  O hear us when we cry to thee
  For all in peril on the sea.

3 O Holy Spirit who didst brood
Upon the waters dark and rude,
And bid their angry tumult cease,
And give, for wild confusion, peace:
  O hear us when we cry to thee
  For all in peril on the sea.

4 O Trinity of love and power,
Our brethren shield in danger's hour;
From rock and tempest them defend,
To safety's harbours them attend;
  O hear us when we cry to thee
  For all in peril on the sea.

William Whiting, 1825–78

27

GENEVA 36 (FIRST STRAIN) *Es sind doch selig (Strassburger Kirchenamt,* 1525)

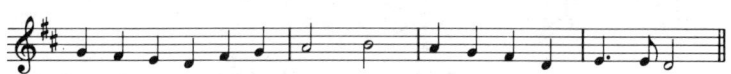

Enrich, Lord, heart, mouth, hands in me,
With faith, with hope, with charity:
That I may run, rise, rest with thee.

George Herbert, 1593–1633

28

TALLIS'S ORDINAL ('9TH TUNE')[1] THOMAS TALLIS, *c.* 1505–85

1 Eternal God, we look to thee,
　　To thee for help we fly;
　Thine eye alone our wants can see,
　　Thy hand alone supply.

2 Lord, let thy fear within us dwell,
　　Thy love our footsteps guide:
　That love will all vain love expel;
　　That fear, all fear beside.

3 Not what we wish, but what we want,[1]
　　O let thy grace supply;
　The good, unasked, in mercy grant;
　　The ill, though asked, deny.

J. Merrick, 1720–69

---

[1] *want* = lack.

29

UFFINGHAM

JEREMIAH CLARK, 1670–1707
Descant, E. P.

With a broad swing

1. Eternal Power, whose high abode
Becomes the grandeur of a God,
Infinite lengths beyond the bounds
Where stars revolve their little rounds:

2. Thee while the first archangel sings
He hides his face behind his wings;
And ranks of shining thrones around
Fall worshipping and spread the ground.

3. Lord, what shall earth and ashes do?
We would adore our Maker too!
From sin and dust to thee we cry,
The Great, the Holy, and the High!

Isaac Watts, 1674–1748, and John Wesley, 1703–91

30

DUNBAR

ARTHUR OLDHAM, 1926–
Commissioned for *The Cambridge Hymnal*

1 Ex-pe-rience does me so in-spire ___ Of this false fail-ing world ___ I tire, ___ That e-ver-more flits

like a vane____ Which to con-sid - - - er is a pain. pain.

1 Experience does me so inspire
  Of this false failing world I tire,
  That evermore flits[1] like a vane
  Which to consider is a pain.

2 And for my cures in sundry place
  With help, Sir, of your noble grace,
  My silly[2] soul shall ne'er be slain
  Nor for such sin to suffer pain.

3 The foremost hope yet that I have
  In all this world, so God me save,
  Is in your grace, both crop and grain,
  Which is a lessening of my pain.

William Dunbar, ? 1465–? 1530
From 'Of the Warldis Instabilitie'

[1] *flits* = wavers.
[2] *silly* = simple, good, poor.

31

ORLANDO GIBBONS, 1583–1625
Descant, E. P.

ANGEL'S SONG (SONG 34)

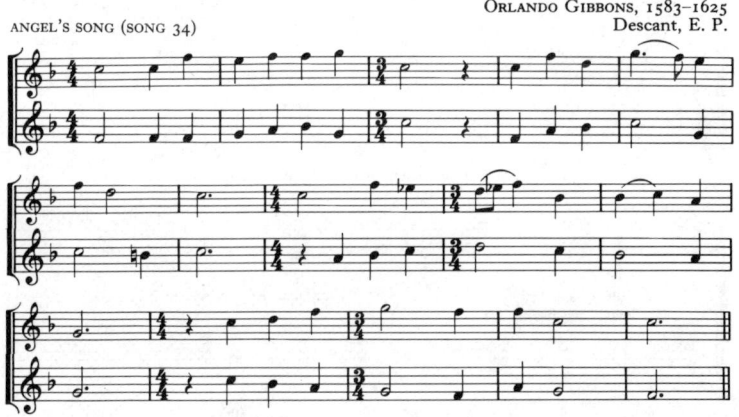

1 Forth in thy name, O Lord, I go,
   My daily labour to pursue;
  Thee, only thee, resolved to know,
   In all I think, or speak, or do.

2 The task thy wisdom hath assigned
   O let me cheerfully fulfil;
  In all my works thy presence find,
   And prove thine acceptable will.

3 Thee may I set at my right hand,
   Whose eyes my inmost substance see,
  And labour on at thy command,
   And offer all my works to thee.

4 Give me to bear thy easy yoke,
   And every moment watch and pray,
  And still to things eternal look,
   And hasten to thy glorious day.

5 For thee delightfully employ
   Whate'er thy bounteous grace hath given,
  And run my course with even joy,
   And closely walk with thee to heaven.

C. Wesley, 1707–88

FISHERMAN PETER

South Carolina Spiritual
Arranged, Elizabeth Poston, 1905–

1. Fisherman Peter on the sea,
   Drop your net, boy, and follow Me!

2. Wrestling Jacob, wrestle on!
   Stop your wrestling and come home!

3. Doubting Thomas, doubt no more!
   Stop your doubting and come home!

Traditional

33

TALLIS'S CANON THOMAS TALLIS, c. 1505–85

1. Glory to thee, my God, this night
   For all the blessings of the light;
   Keep me, O keep me, King of Kings,
   Beneath thine own almighty wings.

2. Forgive me, Lord, for thy dear Son,
   The ill that I this day have done;
   That with the world, myself, and thee,
   I, ere I sleep, at peace may be.

3. Teach me to live, that I may dread
   The grave as little as my bed;
   Teach me to die, that so I may
   Rise glorious at the aweful day.

4. O may my soul on thee repose,
   And may sweet sleep mine eyelids close,
   Sleep that shall me more vigorous make
   To serve my God when I awake.

5. Praise God, from whom all blessings flow;
   Praise him, all creatures here below;
   Praise him above, ye heavenly host;
   Praise Father, Son, and Holy Ghost.

Thomas Ken, 1637–1711

34

TALLIS'S CANON From the version harmonized by BENJAMIN BRITTEN, 1913–

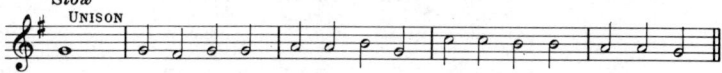

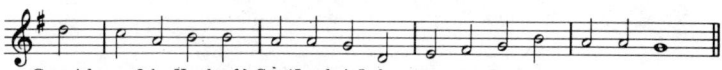

Copyright, 1958 by Hawkes & Son (London) Ltd.

1. The spacious firmament on high
   With all the blue ethereal sky,
   And spangled heavens, a shining frame,
   Their great Original proclaim.
   The unwearied sun from day to day
   Does his Creator's power display,
   And publishes to every land
   The works of an almighty hand.

2. Soon as the evening shades prevail
   The moon takes up the wondrous tale,
   And nightly to the listening earth
   Repeats the story of her birth;
   Whilst all the stars that round her burn,
   And all the planets in their turn,
   Confirm the tidings, as they roll,
   And spread the truth from pole to pole.

3. What though in solemn silence all
   Move round the dark terrestial ball;
   What though nor real voice nor sound
   Amid their radiant orbs be found;
   In reason's ear they all rejoice,
   And utter forth a glorious voice;
   For ever singing as they shine,
   'The hand that made us is Divine.'

Joseph Addison, 1672–1719

35

Proper melody, Plainsong

ADORO TE
Flowing and flexible

1. Godhead here in hiding, whom I do adore
Masked by these bare shadows, shape and nothing more,
See, Lord, at thy service low lies here a heart
Lost, all lost in wonder at the God thou art.

2. Seeing, touching, tasting are in thee deceived;
How says trusty hearing? that shall be believed;
What God's Son hath told me, take for truth I do;
Truth himself speaks truly, or there's nothing true.

3. On the Cross thy Godhead made no sign to men;
Here thy very manhood steals from human ken;
Both are my confession, both are my belief,
And I pray the prayer of the dying thief.

4. I am not like Thomas, wounds I cannot see,
But can plainly call thee Lord and God as he;
This faith each day deeper be my holding of,
Daily make me harder hope and dearer love.

5. O thou our reminder of Christ crucified,
Living Bread, the life of us for whom he died,
Lend this life to me then; feed and feast my mind,
There be thou the sweetness man was meant to find.

6. Jesu, whom I look at shrouded here below,
I beseech thee send me what I long for so,
Some day to gaze on thee face to face in light
And be blest for ever with thy glory's sight.

Ascribed to St. Thomas Aquinas, 1227–74
Translated by Gerard Manley Hopkins, 1844–89

36

MORLICH

WILLIAM WORDSWORTH, 1908–
Commissioned for *The Cambridge Hymnal*

God be in my head,
    and in my understanding;

God be in mine eyes,
    and in my looking;

God be in my mouth,
    and in my speaking;

God be in my heart,
    and in my thinking;

God be at mine end,
    and at my departing.

Horae B.V.M., 'Sarum Primer,' 1514

37

Playford's Psalms, 1671
Tune in the *Scottish Psalter*, 1635
Descant, E.P.

LONDON NEW

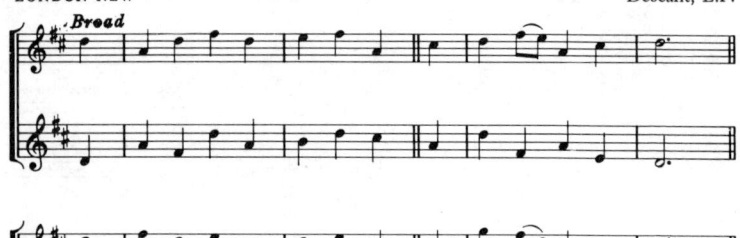

1 God moves in a mysterious way
   His wonders to perform;
He plants his footsteps in the sea,
   And rides upon the storm.

2 Deep in unfathomable mines
   Of never-failing skill
He treasures up his bright designs,
   And works his sovran will.

3 Ye fearful saints, fresh courage take,
   The clouds ye so much dread
Are big with mercy, and shall break
   In blessings on your head.

4 Blind unbelief is sure to err,
   And scan his work in vain;
God is his own interpreter,
   And he will make it plain.

W. Cowper, 1731–1800 .

1 Thy mercy, Lord, is in the heavens,
   Thy truth doth reach the clouds:
Thy justice is like mountains great,
   Thy judgments deep as floods.

2 Lord, thou preservest man and beast,
   How precious is thy grace!
Therefore in shadow of thy wings
   Men's sons their trust shall place.

3 They with the fatness of thy house
   Shall be well satisfied;
From rivers of thy pleasures thou
   Wilt drink to them provide.

4 Because of life the fountain pure
   Remains alone with thee;
And in that purest light of thine
   We clearly light shall see.

5 Thy loving-kindness unto them
   Continue that thee know;
And still on men upright in heart
   Thy righteousness bestow.

Scottish Psalter, 1650, *from Psalm* 36

38

Psalmodia Evangelica, 1789
Descant, E. P.

TRURO
Briskly

1 God of the morning, at whose voice
   The cheerful sun makes haste to rise,
And like a giant doth rejoice
   To run his journey through the skies.

2 From the fair chambers of the east
   The circuit of his race begins;
And, without weariness or rest,
   Round the whole world he flies and
                     shines.

3 Oh! like the sun, may I fulfil
   The appointed duties of the day,
With ready mind and active will
   March on, and keep my heavenly way!

Isaac Watts, 1674–1748

39

LLANFAIR

Melody by ROBERT WILLIAMS, 1781–1821
Descant, E.P.

1 Hail the day that sees him rise,
    Alleluia!
  To his throne above the skies;
    Alleluia!
  Christ, awhile to mortals giv'n,
    Alleluia!
  Enters now the highest heav'n:
    Alleluia!

2 There for him high triumph waits:
  Lift your heads, eternal gates;
  Christ hath conquered death and sin;
  Take the King of glory in:

3 Lo, the heaven its Lord receives,
  Yet he loves the earth he leaves;
  Though returning to his throne,
  Still he calls mankind his own:

4 See, he lifts his hands above;
  See, he shows the prints of love;
  Hark, his gracious lips bestow
  Blessings on his Church below:

5 Still for us he intercedes,
  His prevailing death he pleads,
  Near himself prepares our place,
  He the first-fruits of our race:

6 Lord, though parted from our sight,
  Far above the starry height,
  Grant our hearts may thither rise,
  Seeking thee above the skies:

Charles Wesley, 1707–88
Thomas Cotterill, 1779–1823 and others

40

BOAR'S HILL

LENNOX BERKELEY, 1903–
Commissioned for *The Cambridge Hymnal*

1 Hear'st thou, my soul, what serious things
  Both the Psalm and Sibyl sings
  Of a sure Judge, from whose sharp ray
  The world in flames shall fly away?

2 O that Trump, whose blast shall run
  An even round with the circling sun,
  And urge the murmuring graves to bring
  Pale mankind forth to meet his King!

3 Dear Lord, remember in that day
  Who was the cause thou cam'st this way!
  Thy sheep was strayed, and thou would'st be
  Even lost thyself in seeking me.

4 Shall all that labour, all that cost
  Of love, and even that loss, be lost;
  And this loved soul, judged worth no less
  Than all that way and weariness?

5 Those mercies which thy Mary found,
  And who thy Cross confessed and crowned,
  Hope tells my heart, the same loves be
  Still alive, and still for me.

6 Though both my prayers and tears combine,
  Both worthless are, for they are mine;
  But thou thy bounteous self still be,
  And show thou art, by saving me.

Richard Crashaw, 1613 ?–1649

41

SANTA BARBARA

ARTHUR BLISS, 1891–1975
Commissioned for *The Cambridge Hymnal*

He is the Way.
Follow him through the Land of Unlikeness;
You will see rare beasts and have unique adventures.

He is the Truth.
Seek him in the Kingdom of Anxiety:
You will come to a great city that has expected your return for years.

He is the Life.
Love him in the World of the Flesh:
And at your marriage all its occasions shall dance for joy.

W. H. Auden, 1907–73
From 'The Flight into Egypt' (in 'A Christmas Oratorio')
From 'For the Time Being', 1945

42

ADRIAN BEECHAM, 1904–
Commissioned for *The Cambridge Hymnal*

YELLOW BITTERN

At a moderate pace

1. He wants[1] not friends that hath thy love.
   And may converse and walk with thee,
   And with thy saints here and above,
   With whom for ever I must be.

2. In the communion of the saints
   Is wisdom, safety and delight;
   And when my heart declines and faints,
   It's raisèd by their heat and light!

3. As for my friends, they are not lost;
   The several vessels of thy fleet,
   Though parted now, by tempests tossed,
   Shall safely in the haven meet.

4. Still we are centred all in thee,
   Members, though distant, of one Head;
   In the same family we be,
   By the same faith and spirit led.

5. Before thy throne we daily meet
   As joint petitioners to thee;
   In spirit we each other greet,
   And shall again each other see.

6. The heavenly hosts, world without end,
   Shall be my company above;
   And thou, my best and surest Friend,
   Who shall divide me from thy love?

[1] *wants* = lacks.

R. Baxter, 1615–91

43

HAVELOCK NELSON, 1917–
Adapted from a traditional Irish melody
Commissioned for *The Cambridge Hymnal*

LUTTON

Slow and smooth

1. He shall the broken heart repair,
   And for all sickness and despair
   A cure in Christ provide.

2. And heal the wounded and the bruised,
   His oil into their sores infused,
   And soothing balm applied.

Christopher Smart, 1722–71, from Psalm 147

44

PLUMSTEAD

JOHN JOUBERT, 1927–
Commissioned for *The Cambridge Hymnal*

1. He that is down needs fear no fall,
   He that is low, no pride;
   He that is humble ever shall
   Have God to be his guide.

2. I am content with what I have,
   Little be it, or much:
   And, Lord, contentment still I crave,
   Because thou savest such.

3. Fullness to such, a burden is,
   That go on pilgrimage:
   Here little, and hereafter bliss,
   Is best from age to age.

John Bunyan, 1628–88, from 'The Pilgrim's Progress'

45

SOLOTHURN

Swiss traditional melody
Descant, E.P.

1 How happy is he born and taught,
   'That serveth not another's will;
   Whose armour is his honest thought,
   And simple truth his utmost skill.

2 Whose passions not his masters are;
   Whose soul is still, prepared for death,
   Untied unto the world by care
   Of public fame or private breath;

3 Who God doth late and early pray
   More of his grace than goods to lend;
   And walks with man from day to day
   As with a brother and a friend.

4 This man is freed from servile bands
   Of hope to rise, or fear to fall;
   Lord of himself, though not of lands,
   And, having nothing, yet hath all.

Sir Henry Wotton, 1568–1639

46

DURHAM

Ravenscroft's *Psalter*, 1621
Descant, E. P.

1 How lovely are thy dwellings fair!
   O Lord of Hosts, how dear
   Thy pleasant tabernacles are,
   Where thou dost dwell so near.

2 My soul doth long and almost die
   Thy courts, O Lord, to see;
   My heart and flesh aloud do cry,
   O living God, for thee.

3 There ev'n the sparrow freed from wrong
   Hath found a house of rest,
   The swallow there, to lay her young
   Hath built her brooding nest.

4 Ev'n by thy altars, Lord of Hosts,
   They find their safe abode,
   And home they fly from round the coasts
   Towards thee, my King, my God.

5 Happy who in thy house reside,
   Where thee they ever praise!
   Happy whose strength in thee doth bide,
   And in their hearts thy ways.

6 They journey on from strength to strength
   With joy and gladsome cheer,
   Till all before our God at length
   In Sion do appear.

7 For God, the Lord, both sun and shield,
   Gives grace and glory bright;
   No good from them shall be withheld
   Whose ways are just and right.

J. Milton, 1608–74, *from Psalm* 84

47

TALLIS'S ORDINAL ('9TH TUNE')[1]

THOMAS TALLIS, c. 1505–85
Arranged with variants for festal use by
ELIZABETH POSTON, 1905–

In moderate time, broad

1 How lovely are thy dwellings fair!
　O Lord of Hosts, how dear
Thy pleasant tabernacles are,
　Where thou dost dwell so near.

2 My soul doth long and almost die
　Thy courts, O Lord, to see;
My heart and flesh aloud do cry,
　O living God, for thee.

3 There ev'n the sparrow freed from wrong
　Hath found a house of rest,
The swallow there, to lay her young
　Hath built her brooding nest.

4 Ev'n by thy altars, Lord of Hosts,
　They find their safe abode,
And home they fly from round the coasts
　Towards thee, my King, my God.

5 Happy who in thy house reside,
　Where thee they ever praise!
Happy whose strength in thee doth bide,
　And in their hearts thy ways.

6 They journey on from strength to strength
　With joy and gladsome cheer,
Till all before our God at length
　In Sion do appear.

7 For God, the Lord, both sun and shield,
　Gives grace and glory bright;
No good from them shall be withheld
　Whose ways are just and right.

J. Milton, 1608–74, from Psalm 84

48

OLD 22ND — Melody from Este's *Psalter*, 1592 (also in Day's *Psalter*, 1563)

1 How shall I sing that majesty
    Which angels do admire?
Let dust in dust and silence lie;
    Sing, sing, ye heavenly choir.
Thousands of thousands stand around
    Thy throne, O God most high;
Ten thousand times ten thousand sound
    Thy praise; but who am I?

2 How great a being, Lord, is thine,
    Which doth all beings keep!
Thy knowledge is the only line
    To sound so vast a deep.
Thou art a sea without a shore,
    A sun without a sphere;
Thy time is now and evermore,
    Thy place is ev'rywhere.

John Mason, c. 1645–94

49

STEADFAST

Melody from *Goostly Psalmes and Spirituall Songes*, c. 1546

At a moderate pace, smooth and flexible

UNISON

1 I call on the Lord Jesu Christ, I have none other help but thee. My heart is never set at rest Till thy sweet word have comforted me.

2 A steadfast faith grant me therefore, To hold by thy word evermore. Above all thing, Never resisting But to increase in faith more and more.

1 I call on the Lord Jesu Christ,
 I have none other help but thee.
 My heart is never set at rest
 Till thy sweet word have comforted me.

2 A steadfast faith grant me therefore,
 To hold by thy word evermore.
 Above all thing, never resisting,
 But to increase in faith more and more.

Miles Coverdale, 1487–1568, from 'Goostly Psalmes and Spiritualle Songes', c. 1546,
Queen's College Library, Oxford

50

VATER UNSER

Later form of melody in V. SCHUMANN's *Gesangbuch*, 1539
Version of J.S. BACH, 1685–1750

Slow

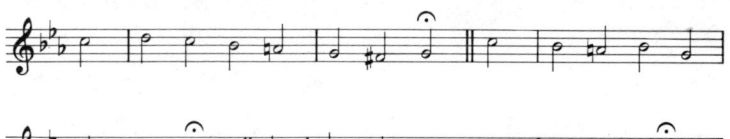

1. If God build not the house, and lay
   The groundwork sure, whoever build,
   It cannot stand one stormy day;
   If God be not the city's shield,
   If he be not their bars and wall,
   In vain the watch-tower, men and all.

2. Though then thou wak'st when others rest,
   Though rising thou prevent'st[1] the sun,
   Though with lean care thou daily feast,
   Thy labour's lost and thou undone;
   But God his child will feed and keep,
   And draw the curtain to his sleep.

   Phineas Fletcher, 1582–1650

[1] *prevent* in the sense of 'go before.'

51

BROOKEND   GUSTAV HOLST, 1874–1934

By kind permission of Miss Imogen Holst and the Trustees of the late Gustav Holst.

1. In this world (the Isle of Dreams),
   While we sit by sorrow's streams,
   Tears and terrors are our themes
                  Reciting:

2. But when once from hence we fly,
   More and more approaching nigh,
   Unto young Eternity
                  Uniting:

3. In that whiter Island, where
   Things are evermore sincere;
   Candour here, and lustre there
                  Delighting:

4. There no monstrous fancies shall
   Out of hell an horror call,
   To create (or cause at all)
                  Affrighting.

5. There in calm and cooling sleep
   We our eyes shall never steep;
   But eternal watch shall keep,
                  Attending

6. Pleasures, such as shall pursue
   Me immortalized, and you;
   And fresh joys, as never to
                  Have ending.

Robert Herrick, 1591–1674

52

PRAYER

EDMUND RUBBRA, 1901–
Commissioned for *The Cambridge Hymnal*

1. Jesus, Lord, that madest me, And with thy blessèd blood hast bought, Forgive that I have grievèd thee With word, with will, and with my thought.

RICHARD DE CASTRE'S PRAYER TO JESUS

1 Jesus, Lord, that madest me,
    And with thy blessèd blood hast bought,
Forgive that I have grievèd thee
    With word, with will, and with my thought.

2 Jesus, grant me my asking,
    Perfect patience in my disease,[1]
And never may I do that thing
    That should thee anywise displease.

3 Jesus, for the deadly tears
    That thou sheddest for my guilt,
Hear and speed my prayers,
    And spare me that I be not spilt.

4 Jesus, keep them that are good,
    Amend them that have grievèd thee,
And send them fruits of earthly food
    As each man needs in his degree.

5 Jesus, that art withouten less
    Almighty God in Trinity,
Cease these wars and send us peace
    With lasting love and charity.

6 Jesus, for thy blessedful[2] blood,
    Bring, if thou wilt, those souls to bliss
From whom I have had any good,
    And spare those that have done amiss.

Lambeth MS., c. 1430, from 'Hymns' (Early English Text Society), ed. Furnivall
Modernized version by David Holbrook.

---

[1] *disease* = dissatisfaction.
[2] *blessedful* = full of blessing.

53

EASTER HYMN Altered 1741 from melody in *Lyra Davidica*, 1708

1 Jesus Christ is risen today,
   Alleluia!
   Our triumphant holy day,
   Alleluia!
   Who did once, upon the cross,
   Alleluia!
   Suffer to redeem our loss.
   Alleluia!

2 Hymns of praise then let us sing
   Unto Christ, our heavenly King,
   Who endured the cross and grave,
   Sinners to redeem and save.

3 But the pains which he endured
   Our salvation have procured,
   Now above the sky he's King,
   Where the angels ever sing.

'*Lyra Davidica,*' 1708, *and the* '*Supplement,*' 1816;
based on '*Surrexit Christus Hodie,*' 14*th century*

54

GALILEE

PHILIP ARMES, 1836–1908
Descant, E. P.

1 Jesus shall reign where'er the sun
  Doth his successive journeys run;
  His kingdom stretch from shore to shore,
  Till moons shall wax and wane no more.

2 People and realms of every tongue
  Dwell on his love with sweetest song,
  And infant voices shall proclaim
  Their early blessings on his name.

3 Blessings abound where'er he reigns;
  The prisoner leaps to lose his chains;
  The weary find eternal rest,
  And all the sons of want are blest.

4 Let every creature rise and bring
  Peculiar honours to our King;
  Angels descend with songs again,
  And earth repeat the loud Amen.

Isaac Watts, 1674–1748, based on Psalm 72

55

GWALCHMAI

J. D. JONES, 1827–70
Descant, E. P.

In moderate time

1. King of glory, King of peace,
     I will love thee;
   And that love may never cease,
     I will move thee.
   Thou hast granted my request,
     Thou hast heard me;
   Thou didst note my working breast,
     Thou hast spared me.

2. Wherefore with my utmost art
     I will sing thee,
   And the cream of all my heart
     I will bring thee.
   Though my sins against me cried,
     Thou didst clear me;
   And alone, when they replied,
     Thou didst hear me.

3. Seven whole days, not one in seven,
     I will praise thee;
   In my heart, though not in heaven,
     I can raise thee.
   Small it is, in this poor sort
     To enrol thee:
   Ev'n eternity's too short
     To extol thee.

George Herbert, 1593–1633

56

HALTON HOLGATE

WILLIAM BOYCE, 1710–79
Descant, E. P.

1 King of mercy, King of love,
   Thou my life, in whom I move,
   Perfect what thou hast begun,
   Let no night put out this sun.

2 Grant I may, my chief desire
   Long for thee, to thee aspire;
   Let my youth, my bloom of days,
   Be my comfort, and thy praise.

3 That hereafter, when I look
   O'er the sullied, sinful book,
   I may find thy hand therein
   Wiping out my shame and sin.

4 O it is thy only art
   To reduce a stubborn heart,
   And since thine is victory,
   Strong holds should belong to thee.

5 Lord, then take it, leave it not
   Unto my dispose or lot;
   Since I would not have it mine,
   O my God, let it be thine.

Henry Vaughan, 1622–95 (slightly altered)

57

DUNDEE

Melody, Scottish Psalter, 1615, Ravenscroft's Psalter, 1621
Descant, E. P.

1 Let saints on earth in concert sing
   With those whose work is done;
   For all the servants of our King
   In earth and heaven are one.

2 One family, we dwell in him,
   One Church, above, beneath;
   Though now divided by the stream,
   The narrow stream of death.

3 One army of the living God,
   To his command we bow;
   Part of his host hath crossed the flood,
   And part is crossing now.

4 E'en now to their eternal home
   There pass some spirits blest,
   While others to the margin come,
   Waiting their call to rest.

5 Jesus, be thou our constant guide;
   Then, when the word is given,
   Bid Jordan's narrow stream divide,
   And bring us safe to heaven.

C. Wesley, 1707–88, and others

58

ST. TEILO

WILLIAM MATHIAS, 1934–
Commissioned for *The Cambridge Hymnal*

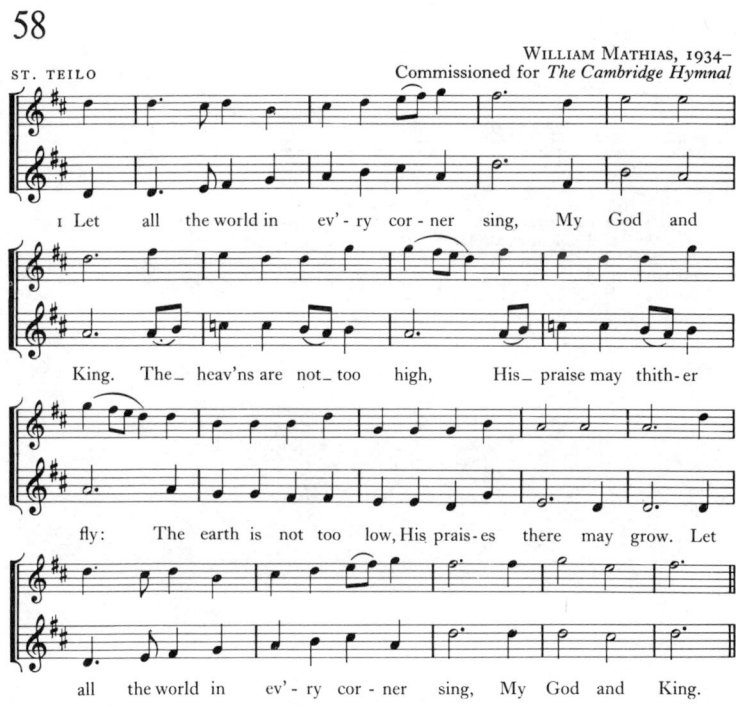

ANTIPHON (I)

1 Let all the world in ev'ry corner sing,
   My God and King.
   The heav'ns are not too high,
   His praise may thither fly:
   The earth is not too low,
   His praises there may grow.
   Let all the world in ev'ry corner sing,
   My God and King.

2 Let all the world in ev'ry corner sing,
   My God and King.
   The church with psalms must shout,
   No door can keep them out;
   But, above all, the heart
   Must bear the longest part.
   Let all the world in ev'ry corner sing,
   My God and King.

George Herbert, 1593–1632

59

MONKLAND

Melody probably by John Antes, 1740–1811
From *Hymn Tunes of the United Brethren*, edited J. Wilkes, 1861
Descant, E.P.

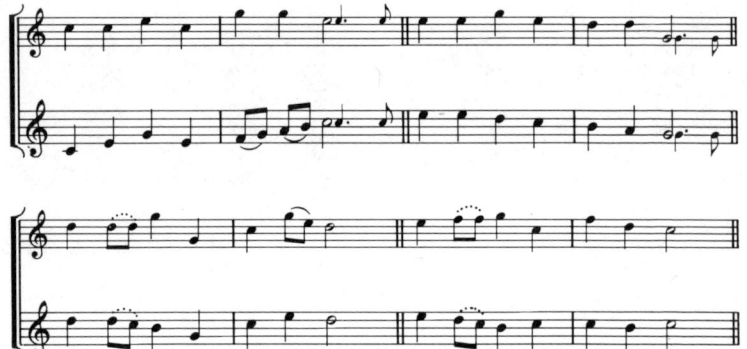

1. Let us with a gladsome mind,
   Praise the Lord, for he is kind:
   For his mercies aye endure,
   Ever faithful, ever sure.

2. Let us blaze his name abroad,
   For of Gods he is the God:
   By his all-commanding might
   Filled the new-made world with light,

3. Caused the golden-tressèd sun
   All day long his course to run;
   The hornèd moon to shine by night,
   'Mongst her spangled sisters bright.

4. He hath, with a piteous eye,
   Looked upon in our misery:
   All living creatures he doth feed,
   And with full hand supplies their need.

5. Let us with a gladsome mind,
   Praise the Lord, for he is kind:
   For his mercies aye endure,
   Ever faithful, ever sure.

John Milton, 1608–74 (altered), from Psalm 136

60

PEERSON

MARTIN PEERSON, 1580–1650
Transcribed and adapted by MARYLIN WAILES
Descant, E.P.

1 Lift up to heav'n, sad wretch, thy heavy sprite,

With acknowledgements to Schott & Co. Ltd.

1 Lift up to heav'n, sad wretch, thy heavy sprite,
   What though thy sins thy due destruction threat?
   The Lord exceeds in mercy as in might:
   His ruth is greater, though thy crimes be great.

2 Repentance needs not fear the heaven's just rod,
   It stays even thunder in the hand of God.
   With cheerful voice to him then cry for grace;
   Thy faith and fainting hope with prayer revive.

3 Remorse for all that truly mourn hath place;
   Not God, but men of him themselves deprive.
   Strive then and he will help. Call him, he'll hear:
   The son needs not the Father's fury fear.

Thomas Campion, 1567–1620

['Most glorious Lord of life,' No. 72, may also be sung to this setting.]

61

WIVETON

LENNOX BERKELEY, 1903–
Commissioned for *The Cambridge Hymnal*

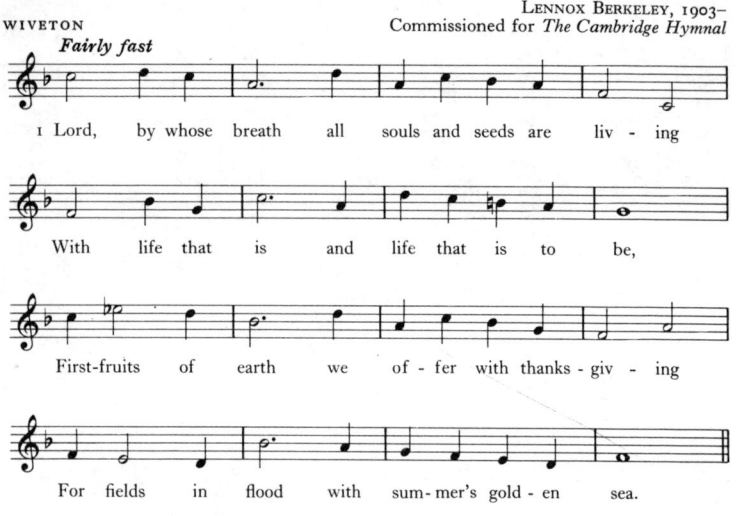

1 Lord, by whose breath all souls and seeds are living
   With life that is and life that is to be,
   First-fruits of earth we offer with thanksgiving
   For fields in flood with summer's golden sea.

2 Lord of the earth, accept these gifts in token
   Thou in thy works art to be all-adored,
   From whom the light as daily bread is broken,
   Sunset and dawn as wine and milk are poured.

3 Poor is our praise, but these shall be our psalter;
   Lo, like thyself they rose up from the dead;
   Lord, give them back when at thy holy altar
   We feed on thee, who art the living bread.

Andrew Young, 1885–1971

62

ERWIN

HERBERT HOWELLS, 1892–
Commissioned for *The Cambridge Hymnal*

1 Lord, by whose breath all souls_ and_ seeds are

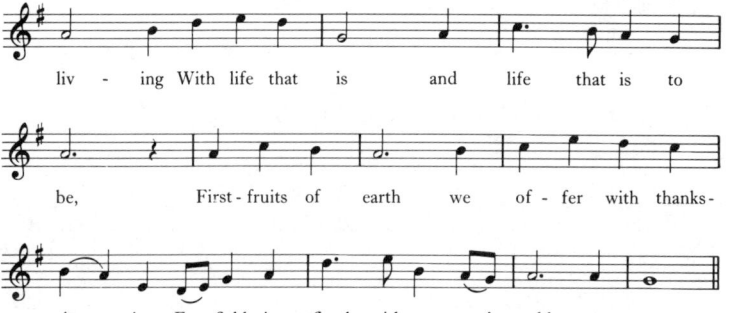

living With life that is and life that is to be, First-fruits of earth we of-fer with thanks- -giv - ing For fields in flood with sum-mer's gold - en sea.

63

COMPTON SCORPION　　　　　　　　　　　　　　ADRIAN BEECHAM, 1904–

At a moderate speed

1 Lord, dismiss us with thy blessing,
　　Fill our hearts with joy and peace;
　Let us each, thy love possessing,
　　Triumph in redeeming grace;
　　　O refresh us, (*twice*)
　Travelling through this wilderness.

2 Thanks we give, and adoration,
　　For thy gospel's joyful sound;
　May the fruits of thy salvation
　　In our hearts and lives abound;
　　　May thy presence (*twice*)
　With us evermore be found.

John Fawcett, 1740–1817

64

WETHERBY

Melody by Samuel Sebastian Wesley, 1810–76
Descant, E.P.

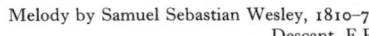

1 Lord, I have made thy word my choice,
   My lasting heritage;
   There shall my noblest powers rejoice,
   My warmest thoughts engage.

2 I'll read the histories of thy love,
   And keep thy laws in sight;
   While through thy promises I rove,
   With ever fresh delight.

3 'Tis a broad land of wealth unknown,
   Where springs of life arise,
   Seeds of immortal bliss are sown,
   And hidden glory lies.

Isaac Watts, 1674–1748

65

SONG 20

ORLANDO GIBBONS, 1583–1625

1 Lord, in the strength of grace,
   With a glad heart and free,
  Myself, my residue of days,
   I consecrate to thee.

2 Thy ransomed servant, I
   Restore to thee thine own;
  And from this moment live or die
   To serve my God alone.

Charles Wesley, 1707–88

66

ASHWELL

EDRIC CUNDELL, 1893–1961
Descant, E. P.

At a moderate speed

1 Lord, it belongs not to my care
   Whether I die or live;
  To love and serve thee is my share,
   And this thy grace must give.

2 If life be long, I will be glad,
   That I may long obey;
  If short, yet why should I be sad
   To welcome endless day?

3 Christ leads me through no darker rooms
   Than he went through before;
  He that into God's kingdom comes
   Must enter by this door.

4 Come, Lord, when grace hath made me meet
   Thy blessèd face to see:
  For if thy work on earth be sweet,
   What will thy glory be!

5 My knowledge of that life is small,
   The eye of faith is dim;
  But 'tis enough that Christ knows all,
   And I shall be with him.

Richard Baxter, 1615–91

67

SOUTHWELL

Damon's *Psalter*, 1579
Descant, E. P.

1 Lord Jesus, think on me
   And purge away my sin;
   From earthborn passions set me free,
   And make me pure within.

2 Lord Jesus, think on me,
   With care and woe oppressed;
   Let me thy loving servant be,
   And taste thy promised rest.

3 Lord Jesus, think on me
   Amid the battle's strife;
   In all my pain and misery.
   Be thou my health and life.

4 Lord Jesus, think on me,
   Nor let me go astray;
   Through darkness and perplexity
   Point thou the heavenly way.

5 Lord Jesus, think on me
   When flows the tempest high:
   When on doth rush the enemy,
   O Saviour, be thou nigh.

6 Lord Jesus, think on me,
   That, when the flood is past,
   I may the eternal brightness see,
   And share thy joy at last.

Synesius, 375–430, translated by A. W. Chatfield, 1808–96

68

ISTE CONFESSOR

Paris Antiphoner, 1681

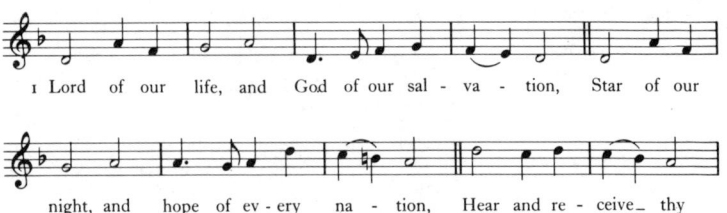

1 Lord of our life, and God of our sal-va-tion, Star of our night, and hope of ev-ery na-tion, Hear and re-ceive thy Church's sup-pli-ca-tion, Lord God Al-migh-ty.

1 Lord of our life, and God of our salvation,
   Star of our night, and hope of every nation,
   Hear and receive thy Church's supplication,
      Lord God Almighty.

2 See round thine ark the hungry billows curling;
   See how thy foes their banners are unfurling;
   Lord, while their darts envenomed they are hurling,
      Thou canst preserve us.

3 Lord, thou canst help when earthly armour faileth,
   Lord, thou canst save when deadly sin assaileth;
   Christ, o'er thy Rock nòr death nor hell prevaileth;
      Grant us thy peace, Lord.

4 Peace in our hearts, our evil thoughts assuaging;
   Peace in thy Church, where brothers are engaging;
   Peace, when the world its busy war is waging:
      Calm thy foes' raging.

5 Grant us thy help till backward they are driven,
   Grant them thy truth, that they may be forgiven;
   Grant peace on earth, and after we have striven,
      Peace in thy heaven.

P. Pusey, 1799–1855, from the German of M. von Löwenstern, 1594–1648

69

ST. VENANTIUS

Poitiers Antiphoner, 1746

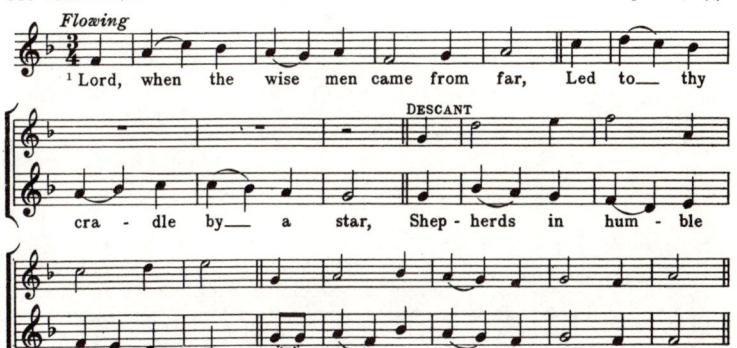

1 Lord, when the wise men came from far,
  Led to thy cradle by a star,
  Shepherds in humble fearfulness
  Walked safely, though their light was less.

2 Wise men in tracing nature's laws
  Ascend unto the highest cause:
  Though wise men better know the way,
  It seems no honest heart can stray.

3 And since no creature comprehends
  The Cause of causes, End of ends,
  He who himself vouchsafes to know
  Best pleases his Creator so.

4 There is no merit in the wise
  But love, the shepherds' sacrifice:
  Wise men, all ways of knowledge past,
  To the shepherds' wonder came at last.

Sidney Godolphin, 1610–43 (altered)

70

HYFRYDOL

Melody by R. PRICHARD, 1811–87
From the version of R. VAUGHAN WILLIAMS, 1872–1958

Slow and dignified

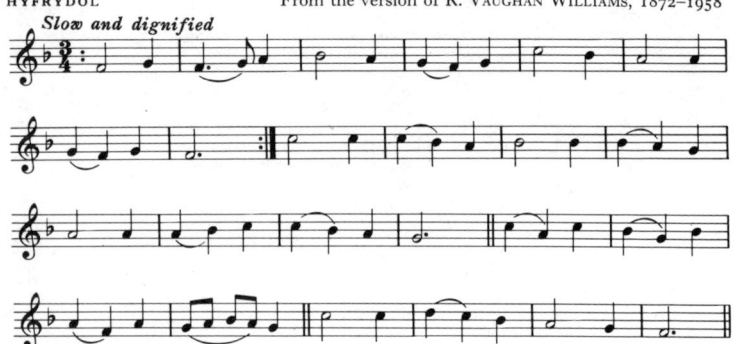

By permission of Oxford University Press

1 Love divine, all loves excelling,
   Joy of heaven, to earth come down,
Fix in us thy humble dwelling,
   All thy faithful mercies crown.
Jesu, thou art all compassion,
   Pure unbounded love thou art;
Visit us with thy salvation,
   Enter every trembling heart.

2 Come, almighty to deliver,
   Let us all thy life receive;
Suddenly return, and never,
   Never more thy temples leave.
Thee we would be always blessing,
   Serve thee as thy hosts above;
Pray, and praise thee without ceasing,
   Glory in thy perfect love.

3 Finish then thy new creation,
   Pure and sinless let us be;
Let us see thy great salvation,
   Perfectly restored in thee,
Changed from glory into glory,
   Till in heaven we take our place,
Till we cast our crowns before thee,
   Lost in wonder, love, and praise.

Charles Wesley, 1707–88

71

JOUISSANCE

Melody by PIERRE BONNET, 1638–1708

Moderately fast (minim beat)

1 Love's re-deem-ing work is done! Al - - - le-lu-ia!
Fought the fight, the bat-tle won: Al - - - le-lu-ia!
Lo, our Sun's e-clipse is o'er! Lo, he sets in blood no more!

1 Love's redeeming work is done!
    Alleluia!
  Fought the fight, the battle won:
    Alleluia!
  Lo, our Sun's eclipse is o'er!
  Lo, he sets in blood no more!

2 Vain the stone, the watch, the seal,
  Christ has burst the gates of hell;
  Death in vain forbids his rise;
  Christ has opened Paradise.

3 Lives again our glorious King;
  Where, O Death, is now thy sting?
  Dying once, he all doth save;
  Where thy victory, O grave?

4 Soar we now where Christ has led,
  Following our exalted Head;
  Made like him, like him we rise;
  Ours the cross, the grave, the skies.

5 Hail the Lord of earth and heaven!
  Praise to thee by both be given:
  Thee we greet triumphant now;
  Hail, the Resurrection thou!

Charles Wesley, 1707–88

72

FARLEY CASTLE

HENRY LAWES, 1596–1662
Descant, E. P.

(repeat this line for last couplet)

1 Most glorious Lord of life, that on this day
    Didst make thy triumph over death and sin,
  And having harrowed hell, didst bring away
    Captivity thence captive, us to win:

2 This joyous day, dear Lord, with joy begin,
    And grant that we for whom thou diddest die,
  Being with thy dear blood clean washed from sin,
    May live for ever in felicity:

3 And that thy love we, weighing worthily,
    May likewise love thee for the same again;
  And for thy sake, that all like dear didst buy,
    With love may one another entertain.

4 So let us love, dear Love, like as we ought;
  Love is the lesson which the Lord us taught.

Edmund Spenser, c. 1552–99

73

Melody by MELCHIOR VULPIUS, c. 1560–1616
Adapted from J.S. BACH, 1685–1750
Descant, E. P.

CHRISTUS DER IST MEIN LEBEN

1 My soul, there is a country
  Far beyond the stars,
  Where stands a wingèd sentry
  All skilful in the wars:

2 There above noise, and danger,
  Sweet peace sits crowned with smiles,
  And one born in a manger
  Commands the beauteous files.

3 He is thy gracious friend,
   And—O my soul, awake!—
   Did in pure love descend,
   To die here for thy sake.

4 If thou canst get but thither,
   There grows the flower of peace,
   The rose that cannot wither,
   Thy fortress and thy ease.

5 Leave then thy foolish ranges,
   For none can thee secure
   But one, who never changes,
   Thy God, thy life, thy cure.

Henry Vaughan, 1622–95

74

Melody by H. ALBERT, 1642
Adapted by J.S. BACH, 1685–1750, in *The Christmas Oratorio*

GOTT DES HIMMELS

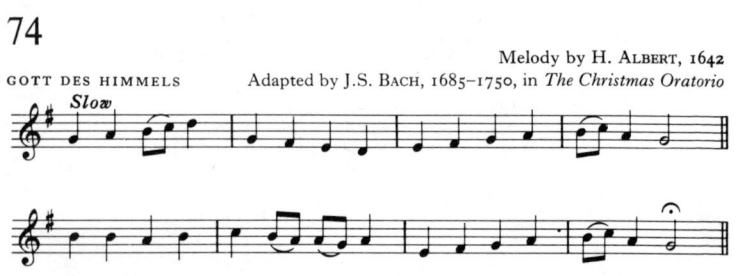

1 May the grace of Christ our Saviour,
   And the Father's boundless love,
With the Holy Spirit's favour,
   Rest upon us from above.

2 Thus may we abide in union
   With each other and the Lord,
And possess, in sweet communion,
   Joys which earth cannot afford.

John Newton, 1725–1807

75

Melody by THOMAS CAMPION, 1567–1620

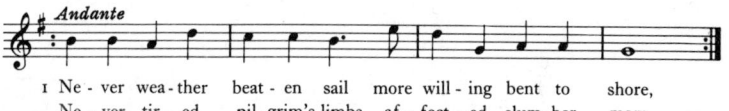

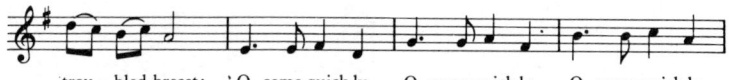

From the transcription by Philip Wilson and Peter Warlock
By permission of Oxford University Press.

1 Never weather-beaten sail more willing bent to shore,
  Never tired pilgrim's limbs affected slumber more
  Than my wearied sprite now longs to fly out of my troubled breast;
  O come quickly, sweetest Lord, and take my soul to rest.

2 Ever blooming are the joys of Heav'n's high paradise,
  Cold age deafs not there our ears, nor vapour dims our eyes;
  Glory there the sun outshines, whose beams the blessed only see;
  O come quickly, glorious Lord, and raise my sprite to thee.

Thomas Campion, 1567–1620

FOR SATURDAY

1 Now's the time for mirth and play,
  Saturday's an holiday!
  Praise to heav'n unceasing yield,
  I've found a lark's nest in the field.

2 A lark's nest? then your play-mate begs
  You'd spare herself and speckled eggs;
  Soon she shall ascend and sing
  Your praises to th' eternal King.

Christopher Smart, 1722–70

77 EVENING HYMN

HENRY PURCELL, 1659–95
Realized by DAVID WILLCOCKS, 1919–
Commissioned for *The Cambridge Hymnal*

Now, now that the sun hath veiled his light, And bid the world good-night; To the soft bed, to the soft, the soft bed my body I dispose, But where, where shall my soul repose? Dear, dear God, e-ven in thy arms, ev'n in thy arms, and can there be An-y so sweet se-cu-ri-ty? can there be An-y so sweet, so sweet se-cu-ri-ty? Then to thy rest,

1 Now that the sun hath veiled his light,
  And bid the world good-night;
  To the soft bed my body I dispose,
  But where, where shall my soul repose?

2 Dear God, even in thy arms, and can there be
  Any so sweet security?
  Then to thy rest, O my soul, and singing, praise
  The mercy that prolongs thy days.

William Fuller, Bishop of Lincoln, 1608–75

78

BON ACCORD *Scottish Psalter* (Aberdeen, 1625)

Brisk and joyful

1. O come, let us sing to the Lord:
   Come, let us every one
   A joyful noise make to the Rock
   Of our salvation.

2. Let us before his presence come
   With praise and thankful voice;
   Let us sing psalms to him with grace,
   And make a joyful noise.

3. For God, a great God and great King
   Above all gods he is.
   Depths of the earth are in his hand,
   The strength of hills is his.

4. To him the spacious sea belongs,
   For he the same did make;
   The dry land also from his hands
   Its form at first did take.

5. O come, and let us worship him,
   Let us bow down withal,
   And on our knees before the Lord
   Our Maker let us fall.

Scottish Psalter, 1615. *From Psalm* 95

79

ST. ANNE

Melody from the *Supplement to the New Version*, 1708
Descant by John Gardner, 1917–
Commissioned for *The Cambridge Hymnal*

1. Our God, our help in ages past,
   Our hope for years to come,
   Our shelter from the stormy blast,
   And our eternal home;

2. Under the shadow of thy throne
   Thy saints have dwelt secure;
   Sufficient is thine arm alone,
   And our defence is sure.

3. Before the hills in order stood,
   Or earth received her frame,
   From everlasting thou art God,
   To endless years the same.

4. A thousand ages in thy sight
   Are like an evening gone,
   Short as the watch that ends the night
   Before the rising sun.

5 Time, like an ever-rolling stream,
  Bears all its sons away;
  They fly forgotten, as a dream
  Dies at the opening day.

6 The busy tribes of flesh and blood,
  With all their cares and fears,
  Are carried downward by the flood,
  And lost in following years.

7 Like flow'ry fields the nations stand,
  Pleased with the morning light:
  The flow'rs beneath the mower's hand
  Lie with'ring ere 'tis night.

8 Our God, our help in ages past,
  Our hope for years to come,
  Be thou our guard while troubles last,
  And our eternal home.

Isaac Watts, 1674–1748. From Psalm 90

80

ST. ANNE
FANFARE

Festal version, with trumpets
Elizabeth Poston, 1905–

81

SONG 67

Melody attributed to ORLANDO GIBBONS, 1583–1625, in
Day's Psalter, 1621
Descant, E. P.

1 O God, my strength and fortitude,
    Of force I must love thee.
  Thou art my castle and defence
    In my necessity.

2 My God, my rock, in whom I trust
    The worker of my wealth,
  My refuge, buckler, and my shield,
    The horn of all my health.

3 I when beset with pain and grief
    Did pray to God for grace;
  And he forthwith heard my complaint,
    Out of his holy place.

4 The Lord descended from above,
    And bowed the heavens high;
  And underneath his feet he cast
    The darkness of the sky.

5 On cherubs and on cherubims
    Full royally he rode;
  And on the wings of mighty winds
    Came flying all abroad.

6 Unspotted are the ways of God,
    His word is purely tried;
  He is a sure defence to such
    As in his faith abide.

7 Most blessèd be the living Lord,
    Most worthy of all praise,
  Who is my rock and saving health—
    Praisèd be he always.

Thomas Sternhold, 1500–1549
From Psalm 18

82

SCHÖNSTER HERR JESU
Melody from the *Münster Gesangbuch*, 1677

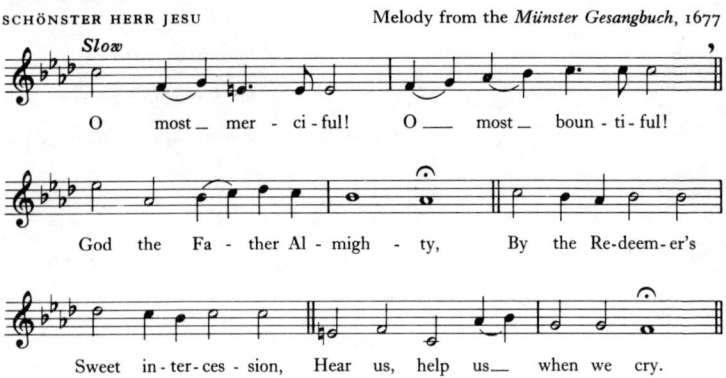

O most merciful!
O most bountiful!
God the Father Almighty,
By the Redeemer's
Sweet intercession,
Hear us, help us when we cry.

Bishop R. Heber, 1783–1826

CHARITY

Arthur Oldham, 1926–
Commissioned for *The Cambridge Hymnal*

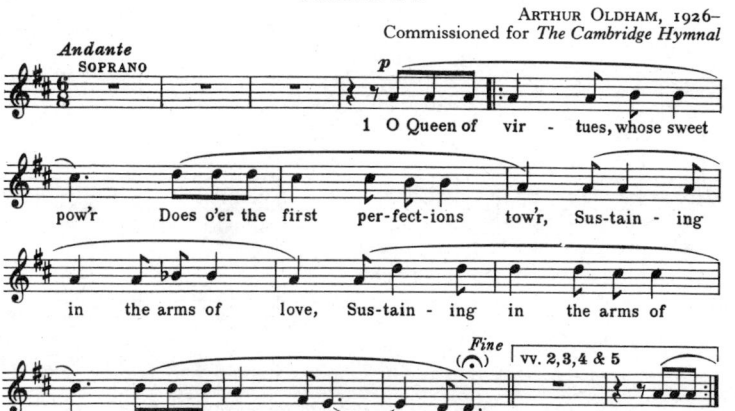

CHARITY

1. O Queen of virtues, whose pow'r
   Does o'er the first perfections tow'r,
   Sustaining in the arms of love   (*sung twice*)
   All want below, all weal above.

2. With thee, O let my thoughts conceive,
   For all the very best believe;
   Predict, pronounce for all the best   (*sung twice*)
   And be by bearing all things blest.

3. To suffer long, and still be kind
   In holy temperance of mind,
   Rejoice that truth is on my side,   (*sung twice*)
   As free from envy as from pride.

4. My cup of water, Christ, is free
   For all that love and thirst for thee;
   With wisdom many a soul to win,   (*sung twice*)
   And loose the irksome bonds of sin.

5. Make me, O Christ, though yet a child,
   To virtue zealous, errors mil'd,
   Profess the feelings of a man,   (*sung twice*)
   And be the Lord's Samaritan.

Christopher Smart, 1722–71

84

PASSION CHORALE

Melody by H. L. HASSLER, 1564–1612
Adapted by J.S. BACH, 1685–1750

1. O sacred head, sore wounded,
　Defiled and put to scorn;
　O kingly head, surrounded
　　With mocking crown of thorn:
　What sorrow mars thy grandeur?
　　Can death thy bloom deflower?
　O countenance whose splendour
　　The hosts of heaven adore!

2. Thy beauty, long-desirèd,
　　Hath vanished from our sight;
　Thy power is all expirèd,
　　And quenched the light of light.
　Ah me! for whom thou diest,
　　Hide not so far thy grace:
　Show me, O Love most highest,
　　The brightness of thy face.

3. I pray thee, Jesus, own me,
　　Me, Shepherd good, for thine;
　Who to thy fold hast won me,
　　And fed with truth divine.
　Me guilty, me refuse not,
　　Incline thy face to me,
　This comfort that I lose not,
　　On earth to comfort thee.

P. Gerhardt, 1607–76,
based on Salve caput cruentatum probably by Arnulf von Loewen, 1200–50
(Paraphrased by the Editors of the Yattendon Hymnal)

J. S. BACH
in the Passion according to St. Matthew

85

HANOVER
DESCANT *for Unison version only*

Attributed to Dr. Croft, 1678–1727
Descant, E.P.

1. O worship the King all glorious above,
   Triumphantly sing his power and his love,
   Our Shield and Defender, the Ancient of days,
   Pavilioned in splendour and girded with praise.

2. O tell of his might, O sing of his grace,
   Whose robe is the light, whose canopy space;
   His chariots of wrath the deep thunderclouds form,
   And dark is his path on the wings of the storm.

3. The earth with its store of wonders untold,
   Almighty, thy power hath founded of old,
   Hath stabilised it fast by a changeless decree,
   And round it hath cast, like a mantle, the sea.

4. Thy bountiful care what tongue can recite?
   It breathes in the air, it shines in the light;
   It streams from the hills, it descends to the plain,
   And sweetly distils in the dew and the rain.

5. Frail children of dust, and feeble as frail,
   In thee do we trust, nor find thee to fail;
   Thy mercies how tender, how firm to the end,
   Our Maker, Defender, Redeemer, and Friend.

6. O measureless Might, ineffable Love,
   While angels delight to hymn thee above,
   Thy humbler creation, though feeble their lays,
   With true adoration shall echo thy praise.

Robert Grant, 1779–1838, based on Psalm 104

86

O FILII ET FILIAE

Proper melody, 17th century, or earlier

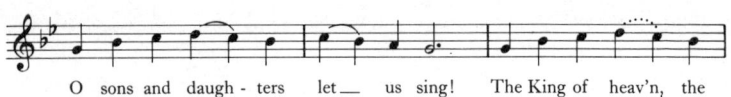

1 *Alleluia! Alleluia! Alleluia!*
  O sons and daughters let us sing!
    The King of heav'n, the glorious King
  O'er death today rose triumphing,
                              Alleluia!

2 That Easter morn at break of day,
    The faithful women went their way
  To seek the tomb where Jesus lay,
                              Alleluia!

3 An angel clad in white they see,
    Who sat and said unto the three,
  'Your lord doth go to Galilee,'
                              Alleluia!

4 How blest are they who have not seen,
    And yet whose faith hath constant been;
  For they eternal life shall have,
                              Alleluia!

5 On this most holy day of days,
    Our hearts and voices, Lord, we raise
  To thee in jubilee and praise,
                              Alleluia!

Jean Tisserand, 1494, translated by J. M. Neale

87

PRAISE, MY SOUL
DESCANT *for use with the harmonization of verse 4*

JOHN GOSS, 1800–80
Descant, E. P.

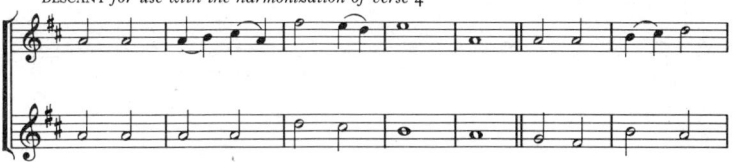

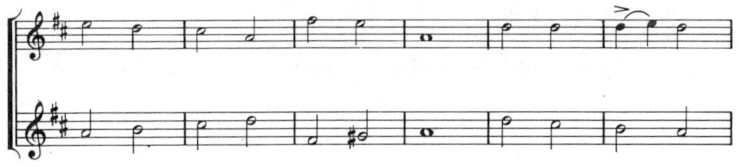

1 Praise, my soul, the King of heaven;
  To his feet thy tribute bring.
 Ransomed, healed, restored, forgiven,
  Who like me his praise should sing?
   Praise him! Praise him!
 Praise the everlasting King!

2 Praise him for his grace and favour
  To our fathers in distress;
 Praise him, still the same for ever,
  Slow to chide, and swift to bless;
   Praise him! Praise him!
 Glorious in his faithfulness.

3 Father-like he tends and spares us;
  Well our feeble frame he knows;
 In his hands he gently bears us,
  Rescues us from all our foes;
   Praise him! Praise him!
 Widely as his mercy flows.

4 Angels, help us to adore him;
  Ye behold him face to face;
 Sun and moon bow down before him,
  Dwellers all in time and space:
   Praise him! Praise him!
 Praise with us the God of grace!

H. F. Lyte, 1793–1847, based on Psalm 103

1 Pleasure it is
To hear, iwis[1]
    The birdès sing.
The deer in the dale,
The sheep in the vale,
    The corn springing;

2 God's purveyance
For sustenance
    It is for man.
Then we always
    To him give praise,
    And thank him than.[2]

William Cornish, d. 1523

[1] *iwis* = I declare.
[2] *than* = then.

89

ELGAR

EDWARD ELGAR, 1857–1934
Adapted, with descant, E. P.

In moderate time

1 Praise to the Ho-li-est in the height, And in the depth be

praise; In all his words most won-der-ful,

Most sure in all his ways.

By permission of Novello & Co. Ltd., Mrs. Elgar Blake and the Elgar Trustees.

1 Praise to the Holiest in the height,
  And in the depth be praise;
In all his words most wonderful,
  Most sure in all his ways.

2 O loving wisdom of our God!
  When all was sin and shame,
A second Adam to the fight
  And to the rescue came.

3 O wisest love! that flesh and blood,
  Which did in Adam fail,
Should strive afresh against the foe,
  Should strive, and should prevail;

4 And that a higher gift than grace
  Should flesh and blood refine,
God's presence and his very Self,
  And essence all-divine.

5 O generous love! that he, who smote
  In Man, for man, the foe,
The double agony in Man
  For man, should undergo.

6 And in the garden secretly,
  And on the cross on high,
Should teach his brethren, and inspire
  To suffer and to die.

7 Praise to the Holiest in the height,
  And in the depth be praise;
In all his words most wonderful,
  Most sure in all his ways.

J. H. Newman, 1801–90

90

YORK

Melody from *Scottish Psalter*, 1615
Descant, E. P.

Moderately slow

1 Pray that Jerusalem may have
  Peace and felicity:
 Let them that love thee and thy peace
  Have still prosperity.

2 Behold how good a thing it is,
  And how becoming well,
 Together such as brethren are
  In unity to dwell.

3 Therefore I wish that peace may still
  Within thy walls remain,
 And ever may thy palaces
  Prosperity retain.

4 Now, for my friends' and brethren's sake,
  Peace be in thee, I'll say;
 And for the house of God our Lord
  I'll seek thy good alway.

5 Within the courts of God's own house,
  Within the midst of thee,
 O City of Jerusalem,
  Praise to the Lord give ye.

Scottish Psalter, 1650. *From Psalms* 122, 133 *and* 116

91

GOPSAL

G.F. HANDEL (adapted), 1685–1759
Descant, E. P.

In moderate time

1 Rejoice! the Lord is King,
  Your Lord and King adore;
Mortals, give thanks and sing,
  And triumph evermore:
    Lift up your heart, lift up your voice;
    Rejoice, again I say, rejoice.

2 Jesus, the Saviour, reigns,
  The God of truth and love;
When he had purged our stains,
  He took his seat above:

3 His kingdom cannot fail;
  He rules o'er earth and heaven;
The keys of death and hell
  Are to our Jesus given:

4 He sits at God's right hand
  Till all his foes submit,
And bow to his command,
  And fall beneath his feet:

C. Wesley, 1707–88

92

Thomas Campion, 1567–1620
Transcribed and edited, E. H. Fellowes, 1870–1951
Descant, E. P.

By permission of Stainer & Bell Ltd.

1 Sing a song of joy,
    Praise our God with mirth.
  His flock who can destroy?
    Is he not Lord of heav'n and earth?

2 Sing we then secure,
    Tuning well our strings,
  With voice as echo pure
    Let us renown the King of Kings.

3 First who taught the day
    From the East to rise?
  Whom doth the sun obey
    When in the seas his glory dies?

4 He the stars directs
    That in order stand.
  Who heaven and earth protects
    But he that framed them with his hand?

5 All that dread his name,
    And his hests[1] observe,
  His arm will shield from shame,
    Their steps from truth shall never
      [swerve.

6 Let us then rejoice,
    Sounding loud his praise,
  So will he hear our voice,
    And bless on earth our peaceful days.

[1] *hests* = behests, commands.

Thomas Campion, 1567–1620

93

OFFERTORIUM MICHAEL HAYDN, 1737–1806

1 Sometimes a light surprises
  The Christian while he sings:
 It is the Lord who rises
  With healing in his wings;
 When comforts are declining,
 He grants the soul again
 A season of clear shining
 To cheer it after rain.

2 In holy contemplation
  We sweetly then pursue
 The theme of God's salvation,
  And find it ever new:
 Set free from present sorrow,
 We cheerfully can say,
 E'en let the unknown morrow
 Bring with it what it may.

3 It can bring with it nothing
  But he will bear us through;
 Who gives the lilies clothing
  Will clothe his people too:
 Beneath the spreading heavens
 No creature but is fed;
 And he who feeds the ravens
 Will give his children bread.

4 Though vine nor fig-tree neither
  Their wonted fruit should bear,
 Though all the fields should wither,
  Nor flocks nor herds be there;
 Yet, God the same abiding,
 His praise shall tune my voice;
 For, while in him confiding,
 I cannot but rejoice.

W. Cowper, 1731–1800

94

ST. ETHELWALD Tune by WILLIAM HENRY MONK, 1823–89

Alla marcia
UNISON

1 Sol-diers of Christ, a-rise, And put your ar-mour on; Strong
in the strength which God sup-plies, Through his e-ter-nal Son;

2 Strong in the Lord of hosts, And in his might-y pow'r; Who

1. Soldiers of Christ, arise,
   And put your armour on;
   Strong in the strength which God supplies,
   Through his eternal Son;

2. Strong in the Lord of hosts,
   And in his mighty power;
   Who in the strength of Jesus trusts
   Is more than conqueror.

3. Stand, then, in his great might,
   With all his strength endued;
   And take, to arm you for the fight,
   The panoply of God.

4. To keep your armour bright
   Attend with constant care,
   Still walking in your Captain's sight,
   And watching unto prayer.

5. From strength to strength go on;
   Wrestle and fight and pray;
   Tread all the powers of darkness down,
   And win the well-fought day.

6. That, having all things done,
   And all your conflicts past,
   Ye may o'ercome, through Christ alone,
   And stand entire at last.

Charles Wesley, 1707–88; based on Ephesians, vi, 10–18

95 (continued)

1. Suddenly afraid, half-waking, half-sleeping,
   And greatly dismayed, a woman sat weeping,
   With favour in her face far passing my reason,
   And of her sore weeping this was the occasion:
   Her son in her lap lay, she said, slain by treason,
   If weeping might ripe be, it seemed then in season.
       Jesus, so she sobbèd,
       Her son was bobbèd[1]
       And of his life robbèd;
           Saying these words as I say thee,
           'Who cannot weep, come learn of me.'

2. I said I could not weep, I was so hard-hearted.
   She answered me shortly with words that smarted:
   'Lo, nature shall move thee; thou must be converted,
   Thine own Father this night is dead:' this she retorted;
       Jesus my son is bobbèd,
       And of his life robbèd,
       For sooth then I sobbèd;
           Verifying these words, saying to thee,
           'Who cannot weep, come learn of me.'

3. 'Now break heart I pray thee! this cord cuts so cruelly,
   So beaten, so wounded, ill-treated so foully;
   What man can behold, and weep not? None, truly,
   So see my dead dear son bleeding thus newly!'
       Ever still she sobbèd,
       So her son was bobbèd,
       And of his life robbèd;
           Repeating these words as I say thee,
           'Who cannot weep, come learn of me.'

4. On me she cast her eyes and said, 'See, man, thy brother!'
   She kissed him and said, 'Sweet, am I not thy mother?'
   And swooning she fell; in this state would be neither;
   I knew not which was more like death, the one or the other.
       Yet she revived and sobbèd
       How her son was bobbèd
       And of his life robbèd.
           'Who cannot weep,' this is her lay,
           And with those words she vanishèd away.

Medieval MS. in the Library of Trinity College, Cambridge (MS. 0.9.38)
printed in Hymns (Early English Text Society), ed. Furnivall
Modernized version by David Holbrook.

[1] *bobbèd* = beaten.

96

PEN SELWOOD

ARTHUR BLISS, 1891–1975
Commissioned for *The Cambridge Hymnal*

1 Sweet day, so cool, so calm, so bright, The bri-dal of the earth and sky,—— The dew shall

1 Sweet day, so cool, so calm, so bright,
   The bridal of the earth and sky,
 The dew shall weep thy fall tonight;
   For thou must die.

2 Sweet rose, whose hue, angry and brave,
   Bids the rash gazer wipe his eye,
 Thy root is ever in its grave,
   And thou must die.

3 Sweet spring, full of sweet days and roses,
   A box where sweets compacted lie,
 My music shows you have your closes,
   And all must die.

4 Only a sweet and virtuous soul,
   Like seasoned timber, never gives;
 But, though the whole world turn to coal,
   Then chiefly lives.

George Herbert, 1593-1633

97

FESHIE

WILLIAM WORDSWORTH, 1908–
Commissioned for *The Cambridge Hymnal*

1. Sweet Infancy!
   O heavenly fire! O sacred light!
   How fair and bright!
   How great am I
   Whom the whole world doth magnify!

2. O heavenly joy!
   O great and sacred blessedness
   Which I possess!
   So great a joy
   Who did into my arms convey?

3. From God above
   Being sent, the gift doth me enflame
   To praise his name;
   The stars do move,
   The sun doth shine, to show his love.

4. O how divine
   Am I! To all this sacred wealth,
   This life and health,
   Who raised? Who mine
   Did make the same? What hand divine!

Thomas Traherne, 1637–74

98 SIDNEY'S TWENTY-THIRD PSALM

SPEYSIDE

WILLIAM WORDSWORTH, 1908–
Commissioned for *The Cambridge Hymnal*
Descant, E. P.

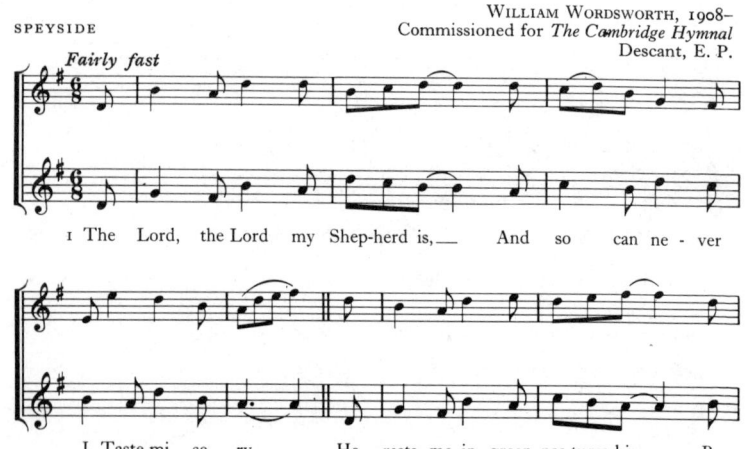

wa-ters still and sweet He guides my feet.

1. The Lord, the Lord my Shepherd is,
And so can never I
Taste misery.
He rests me in green pastures his:
By waters still and sweet
He guides my feet.

2. He me revives; leads me the way
Which righteousness doth take,
For his name sake.
Yea, though I should through valleys stray
Of death's dark shade, I will
No whit fear ill.

3. For thou, dear Lord, thou me beset'st;
Thy rod and thy staff be
To comfort me:
Before me thou a table set'st
Even when foe's envious eye
Doth it espy.

4. Thou oil'st my head, thou fill'st my cup,
Nay, more, thou endless good,
Shall give me food:
To thee, I say, ascended up,
Where thou, the Lord of all,
Dost hold thy hall.

Sir Philip Sidney, 1554–86. From Psalm 23

99   HERBERT'S TWENTY-THIRD PSALME

UNIVERSITY

?JOHN RANDALL, 1715–99
Descant, E. P.

1. The God of love my Shepherd is,
And he that doth me feed;
While he is mine and I am his,
What can I want or need?

2. He leads me to the tender grass,
Where I both feed and rest;
Then to the streams that gently pass:
In both I have the best.

3. Or if I stray, he doth convert,
And bring my mind in frame;
And all this not for my desert,
But for his holy name.

4. Yea, in death's shady black abode
Well may I walk, not fear;
For thou art with me; and thy rod
To guide, thy staff to bear.

5. Nay, thou dost make me sit and dine,
Ev'n in my enemies' sight:
My head with oil, my cup with wine
Runs over day and night.

6. Surely thy sweet and wondrous love
Shall measure all my days;
And, as it never shall remove,
So neither shall my praise.

George Herbert, 1593–1633. From Psalm 23

100

SURREY
HENRY CAREY, c. 1690–1743

Flowing

1 The Lord my pasture shall prepare,
    And feed me with a shepherd's care;
    His presence shall my wants supply,
    And guard me with a watchful eye;
    My noonday walks he shall attend,
    And all my midnight hours defend.

2 When in the sultry glebe I faint,
    Or on the thirsty mountain pant,
    To fertile vales and dewy meads
    My weary wandering steps he leads,
    Where peaceful rivers, soft and slow,
    Amid the verdant landscape flow.

3 Though in a bare and rugged way
    Through devious lonely wilds I stray,
    Thy bounty shall my pains beguile;
    The barren wilderness shall smile
    With sudden greens and herbage crowned,
    And streams shall murmur all around.

4 Though in the paths of death I tread,
    With gloomy horrors overspread,
    With steadfast heart shall fear no ill,
    For thou, O Lord, art with me still:
    Thy friendly crook shall give me aid,
    And guide me through the dreadful shade.

Joseph Addison, 1672–1719. From Psalm 23

101   HERBERT'S TWENTY-THIRD PSALME

BICCLESCOMBE
JOHN GARDNER, 1917–
Commissioned for *The Cambridge Hymnal*

♩. = 52
DESCANT *(verses 3 & 4 or 5 & 6)*

1 The God of love my Shep-herd is, And he that

1. The God of love my Shepherd is,
   And he that doth me feed;
   While he is mine and I am his,
   What can I want or need?

2. He leads me to the tender grass,
   Where I both feed and rest;
   Then to the streams that gently pass:
   In both I have the best.

3. Or if I stray, he doth convert,
   And bring my mind in frame;
   And all this not for my desert,
   But for his holy name.

4. Yea, in death's shady black abode
   Well may I walk, not fear;
   For thou art with me, and thy rod
   To guide, thy staff to bear.

5. Nay, thou dost make me sit and dine,
   Ev'n in my enemies' sight:
   My head with oil, my cup with wine
   Runs over day and night.

6. Surely thy sweet and wondrous love
   Shall measure all my days;
   And, as it never shall remove,
   So neither shall my praise.

George Herbert, 1593–1633. *From Psalm* 23

1 My Shepherd will supply my need,
  Jehovah is his name;
In pastures fresh he makes me feed
  Beside the living stream.

2 He brings my wand'ring spirit back
  When I forsake his ways:
He leads me for his mercy's sake
  In paths of truth and grace.

3 When I walk through the shades of death
  Thy presence is my stay;
One word of thy supporting breath
  Drives all my fears away.

4 Thy hand, in sight of all my foes
  Doth still my table spread;
My cup with blessings overflows,
  Thy oil anoints my head.

5 The sure provisions of my God
  Attend me all my days;
O may thy house be my abode
  And all thy works my praise.

6 There would I find a settled rest,
  Where others go and come;
No more a stranger or a guest,
  But like a child at home.

Isaac Watts, 1674-1748. From Psalm 23
Printed in 'The Southern Harmony and Musical Companion' by
William Walker (New York, 1854)

103

CRIMOND

Melody by JESSIE SEYMOUR IRVINE, 1836-1887
Descant, E.P.

1 The Lord's my Shepherd, I'll not want;
    He makes me down to lie
  In pastures green: he leadeth me
    The quiet pastures by.

2 My soul he doth restore again;
    And me to walk doth make
  Within the paths of righteousness,
    Ev'n for his own name's sake.

3 Yea, though I walk in death's dark vale,
    Yet will I fear none ill:
  For thou art with me; and thy rod
    And staff me comfort still.

4 My table thou hast furnishèd
    In presence of my foes;
  My head thou dost with oil anoint,
    And my cup overflows.

5 Goodness and mercy all my life
    Shall surely follow me:
  And in God's home for evermore
    My dwelling-place shall be.

Scottish Psalter, 1650. From Psalm 23

104

SANDYS

English traditional carol melody
From W. Sandys *Christmas Carols, Ancient and Modern*, 1833
Descant, E.P.

1. Teach me, my God and King,
   In all things thee to see,
   And what I do in anything
   To do it as for thee.

2. A man that looks on glass,
   On it may stay his eye;
   Or if he pleaseth, through it pass,
   And then the heaven espy.

3. All may of thee partake;
   Nothing can be so mean,
   Which with this tincture, 'for thy sake',
   Will not grow bright and clean.

4. A servant with this clause
   Makes drudgery divine;
   Who sweeps a room, as for thy laws,
   Makes that and the action fine.

5. This is the famous stone
   That turneth all to gold;
   For that which God doth touch and own
   Cannot for less be told.

George Herbert, 1593–1633. *The Elixir*

105

TE LUCIS

Plain-chant melody from *Andernach Gesangbuch*

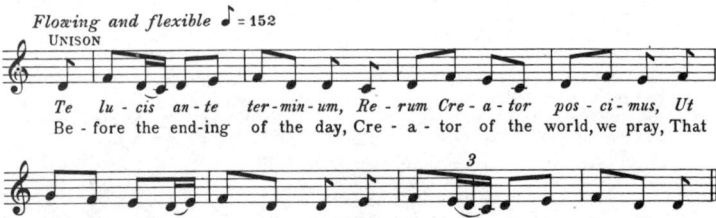

Te lu-cis an-te ter-min-um, Re-rum Cre-a-tor pos-ci-mus, Ut pro tu-a cle-men-ti-a, Sis prae-sul et cus-to-di-a.
Be-fore the end-ing of the day, Cre-a-tor of the world, we pray, That thou with wont-ed love would'st keep Thy watch a-round us while we sleep.

ST. AMBROSE

SECOND TUNE

From LA FEILLÉE, *Méthode du plain-chant,* 1782

1. Te lucis ante terminum,
   Rerum Creator poscimus,
   Ut pro tua clementia,
   Sis praesul et custodia.

2. Praesta, Pater piissime,
   Patrique compar unice,
   Cum Spiritu Paraclito
   Regnans per omne saeculum.

   Before 8th century.

1. Before the ending of the day,
   Creator of the world, we pray
   That thou with wonted love would'st keep
   Thy watch around us while we sleep.

2. Almighty Father, hear our cry,
   Through Jesus Christ, our Lord most high,
   Who, with the Holy Ghost and thee
   Doth live and reign eternally.

   Version from Wells Office Book, by permission
   (Both versions abbreviated by the Editors)

106   THAT VIRGIN'S CHILD

LINDENS

EDMUND RUBBRA, 1901–
Commissioned for *The Cambridge Hymnal*

THAT VIRGIN'S CHILD

1. That virgin's child
   Most meek and mild,
   Alonely for my sake,
   His father's will
   For to fulfil
   He came great pains to take.

2. Such pain and smart
   As in his heart
   He suffered for mankind
   Can no man take,
   Nor mourning make
   So meekly for his friend.

3. Now Christ Jesu,
   Of love most true,
   Have mercy upon me:
   I ask thee grace
   For my trespass,
   That I have done to thee.

4. For thy sweet name
   Save me from shame
   And all adversity:
   For Mary's sake
   To thee me take,
   And mourn no more for me.

   John Gwyneth, c. 1530

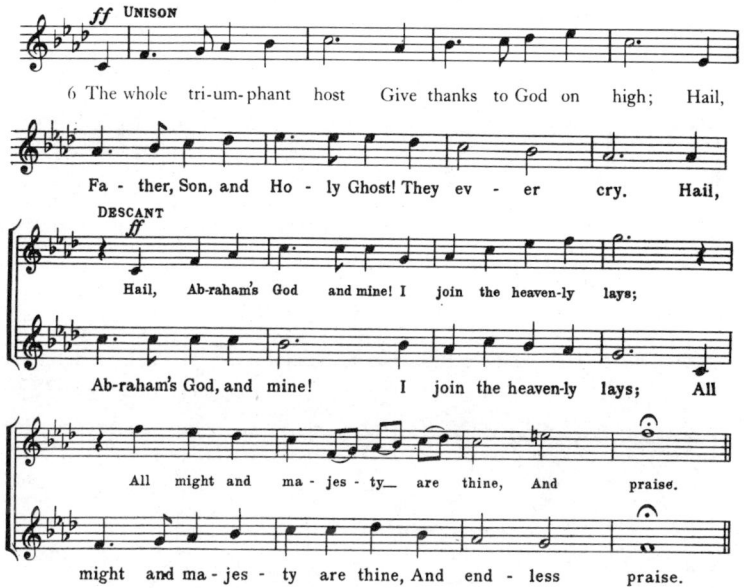

1. The God of Abraham praise,
   Who reigns enthroned above,
   Ancient of everlasting days,
      And God of love.
   Jehovah! Great I AM!
   By earth and heaven confessed;
   I bow and bless the sacred name
      For ever blessed.

2. The God of Abraham praise,
   At whose supreme command
   From earth I rise, and seek the joys
      At his right hand.
   I all on earth forsake—
   Its wisdom, fame and power—
   And him my only portion make,
      My shield and tower.

3. The goodly land we see,
   With peace and plenty blest:
   A land of sacred liberty
      And endless rest;
   There milk and honey flow,
   And oil and wine abound,
   The trees of life for ever grow,
      With mercy crowned.

4. He by himself hath sworn,
   I on his oath depend:
   I shall, on eagles' wings upborne,
      To heaven ascend;
   I shall behold his face,
   I shall his power adore,
   And sing the wonders of his grace
      For evermore.

5. The God who reigns on high,
   The great archangels sing;
   And Holy, holy, holy, cry,
      Almighty King.
   Who was and is the same,
   And evermore shall be;
   Jehovah, Father, Great I AM,
      We worship thee.

6. The whole triumphant host
   Give thanks to God on high;
   Hail, Father, Son, and Holy Ghost!
      They ever cry.
   Hail, Abraham's God, and mine!
   I join the heavenly lays;
   All might and majesty are thine,
      And endless praise.

*Thomas Olivers, 1725–99
based on the Yigdal*

108

JENA (DAS NEUGEBORNE KINDLEIN)

Melody from VULPIUS's *Gesangbuch* (Jena, 1609)
Descant, E.P.

1 The holy Son of God most high,
   For love of Adam's lapsèd race,
Quit the sweet pleasures of the sky
   To bring us to that happy place.

2 His robes of light he laid aside,
   Which did his majesty adorn,
And the frail state of mortals tried,
   In human flesh and figure born.

3 Whole choirs of angels loudly sing
   The mystery of his sacred birth;
And the blest news to shepherds bring,
   Filling their watchful souls with mirth.

4 The Son of God thus man became,
   That men the sons of God might be,
And by their second birth regain
   A likeness to his deity.

Henry More, 1614–87

109

OLD 107TH

Melody in the *Scottish Psalter*, 1635
Descant, E.P.

1 The Lord will come, and not be slow,
His footsteps cannot err;
Before him righteousness shall go,
His royal harbinger.

2 For lo thy furious foes now swell
And storm outrageously,
And they that hate thee, proud and fell,
Exalt their heads full high.

3 My God, O make them as a wheel
No quiet let them find,
Giddy and restless let them reel
Like stubble from the wind.

4 As when an aged wood takes fire
Which on a sudden strays,
The greedy flame runs higher and higher
Till all the mountains blaze.

5 So with thy whirlwind them pursue,
And with thy tempest chase;
And till they yield thee honour due,
Lord, fill with shame their face.

6 Truth from the earth, like to a flower,
Shall bud and blossom then;
And justice from her heavenly bower,
Look down on mortal men.

7 Rise, God, judge thou the earth in might,
This wicked earth redress;
For thou art he who shalt by right
The nations all possess.

8 The nations all whom thou hast made
Shall come, and all shall frame
To bow them low before thee, Lord,
And glorify thy name.

9 For great thou art, and wonders great
By thy strong hand are done:
Thou in thy everlasting seat
Remainest God alone.

John Milton, 1608–74. *Based on Psalms* 82, 85, 86

110

OAKLEY
R. Vaughan Williams, 1872–1958

By permission, Oxford University Press

1 The night is come; like to the day
Depart not thou, great God away;
Let not my sins, black as the night,
Eclipse the lustre of thy light.
    Thou, whose nature cannot sleep,
    On my temples sentry keep;
    Make my sleep a holy trance;
    While I rest, my soul advance.

2 So may I then, my rest being wrought,
Awake into some holy thought,
And with as active vigour run
My course as doth the nimble sun.
    Sleep's a death: O make me try
    Sleeping, what it is to die!
    Come the hour when I shall never
    Sleep again, but wake for ever!

Sir Thomas Browne (altered), 1605–82

111 JESUS CHRIST THE APPLE TREE

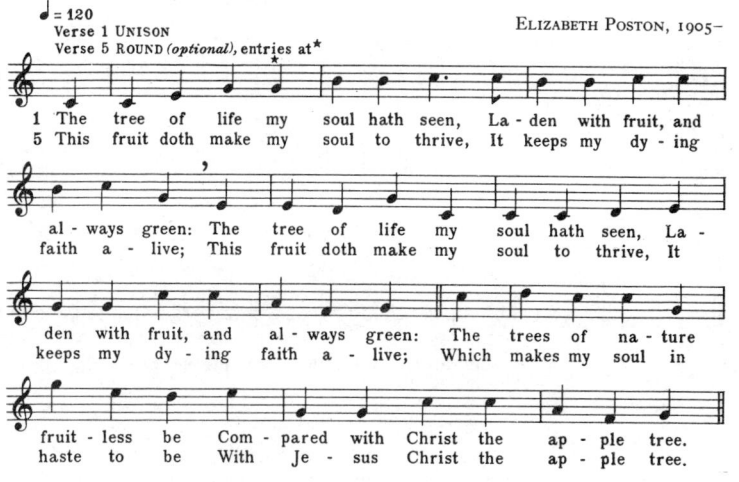

JESUS CHRIST THE APPLE TREE

1 The tree of life my soul hath seen,
  Laden with fruit, and always green: } *twice*
  The trees of nature fruitless be
  Compared with Christ the apple tree.

2 His beauty doth all things excel:
  By faith I know, but ne'er can tell } *twice*
  The glory which I now can see
  In Jesus Christ the apple tree.

3 For happiness I long have sought,
  And pleasure dearly I have bought: } *twice*
  I missed of all; but now I see
  'Tis found in Christ the apple tree.

4 I'm weary with my former toil,
  Here I will sit and rest awhile: } *twice*
  Under the shadow I will be,
  Of Jesus Christ the apple tree.

5 This fruit doth make my soul to thrive,
  It keeps my dying faith alive; } *twice*
  Which makes my soul in haste to be
  With Jesus Christ the apple tree.

Anon, collection of Joshua Smith, New Hampshire, 1784

112

ST. MAGNUS (NOTTINGHAM)

Probably by JEREMIAH CLARK, 1670–1707
Descant, E. P.

1 The head that once was crowned with thorns
  Is crowned with glory now:
A royal diadem adorns
  The mighty Victor's brow.

2 The highest place that heaven affords
  Is his, is his by right,
The King of kings and Lord of lords,
  And heaven's eternal Light;

3 The joy of all who dwell above,
  The joy of all below,
To whom he manifests his love,
  And grants his name to know.

4 To them the cross, with all its shame,
  With all its grace is given:
Their name an everlasting name,
  Their joy the joy of heaven.

T. Kelly, 1760–1854

113 THE WATER STOOD LIKE WALLS OF BRASS

ST. OLAF'S

JOHN GARDNER, 1917–
Commissioned for *The Cambridge Hymnal*

1 The water stood like walls of brass, To let the sons of Is-rael pass; And from the rock in rivers burst, At Moses' prayer to quench their thirst.

1 The water stood like walls of brass,
  To let the sons of Israel pass;
  And from the rock in rivers burst,
  At Moses' prayer to quench their thirst.

2 The fire restrained by God's commands,
  Could only burn his people's bands;
  Too faint, when he was with them there,
  To singe their garments or their hair.

3 At Daniel's feet the lions lay
  Like harmless lambs, nor touched their prey;
  And ravens, which on carrion fed,
  Procured Elijah flesh and bread.

4 Thus creatures only can fulfil
  Their great Creator's holy will;
  And when his servants need their aid
  His purposes must be obeyed.

5 So if his blessing he refuse,
  Their pow'r to help they quickly lose,
  Sure as on creatures we depend,
  Our hopes in disappointment end.

6 Then let us trust the Lord alone,
  And creature-confidence disown;
  Nor if they threaten need we fear,
  They cannot hurt if he be near.

7 If instruments of pain they prove,
  Still are they guided by his love;
  As lancets by the surgeon's skill,
  Which wound to cure, and not to kill.

John Newton, 1725–1807

114

LÖWENSTERN (HEUT' IST O MENSCH)   M. VON LÖWENSTERN, 1594–1648

1 Thou art my Life: if thou but turn a - way

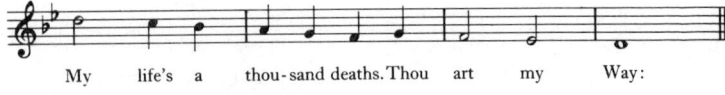
My life's a thou-sand deaths. Thou art my Way:

With - out thee, Lord, I tra - vel not, but stray.

1 Thou art my Life: if thou but turn away
My life's a thousand deaths. Thou art my Way:
Without thee, Lord, I travel not, but stray.

2 My Light thou art: without thy glorious sight
My eyes are darkened with perpetual night.
My God, thou art my Way, my Life, my Light.

3 Thou art my Way: I wander, if thou fly.
Thou art my Light: if hid, how blind am I!
Thou art my Life: if thou withdraw, I die.

4 Disclose thy sunbeams; close thy wings and stay;
See, see how I am blind, and dead, and stray,
O thou that art my Light, my Life, my Way!

Francis Quarles, 1592–1644

115

THE GENTLE PATH   ELIZABETH POSTON, 1905–

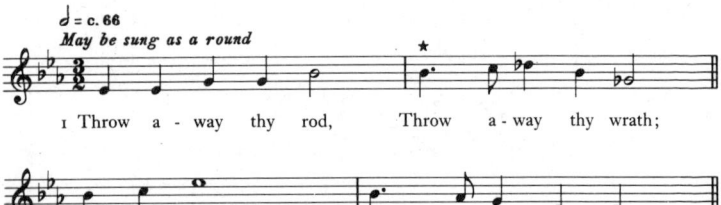
1 Throw a - way thy rod, Throw a - way thy wrath;
O my God, Take the gen - tle path!

1 Throw away thy rod,
　Throw away thy wrath;
　　O my God,
　Take the gentle path!

2 For my heart's desire
　Unto thine is bent:
　　I aspire
　To a full consent.

3 Then let wrath remove;
　Love will do the deed:
　　For with Love
　Stony hearts will bleed.

4 Throw away thy rod;
　Though man frailties hath,
　　Thou art God:
　Throw away thy wrath!

　　　　　　　　　George Herbert, 1593–1633

116

THIRD MODE MELODY

THOMAS TALLIS, *c.* 1515–85
(Rhythm slightly simplified)

1 Thou wast, O God, and thou wast blest,
　Before the world began;
Of thine eternity possessed
　Before time's hour-glass ran.
Thou needest none thy praise to sing,
　As if thy joy could fade;
Could'st thou have needed anything,
　Thou could'st have nothing made.

2 Great and good God, it pleased thee
　Thy Godhead to declare;
And what thy goodness did decree
　Thy greatness did prepare;
Thou spak'st, and heav'n and earth appeared,
　And answered to thy call;
As if their maker's voice they heard,
　Which is the creature's all.

3 To whom, Lord, should I sing, but thee,
　　The maker of my tongue?
　Lord, other lords would seize on me,
　　But I to thee belong.
　As waters haste into the sea,
　　And earth into its earth,
　So let my soul return to thee,
　　From whom it had its birth.

　　　　　　　　　John Mason, c. 1645–94

117 SIMPLE GIFTS
(SHAKER SONG)

Adapted by
AARON COPLAND, 1900–

*To be sung freely, without rigid adherence to strict rhythm.

© Copyright 1950 by Aaron Copland
Reprinted by permission of the sole publishers, Boosey & Hawkes Music Publishers Ltd.

1. 'Tis the gift to be simple, 'tis the gift to be free,
   'Tis the gift to come down where you ought to be,
   And when we find ourselves in the place just right,
   'Twill be in the valley of love and delight.

2. When true simplicity is gained,
   To bow and to bend we shan't be ashamed;
   To turn, turn will be our delight
   Till by turning, turning we come round right.

Song of the Shaker sect (American, 1837–47)

The following may be used as alternative second verse:

When true simplicity is gained,
To bow and to bend we shan't be ashamed;
We'll worship and bow down, we will rejoice
When we hear the Shepherd's gentle voice.

From a Shaker Hymnal in manuscript.
See 'Hymns as Poetry', Ingram and Newton (Constable, 1956)

118

BISHOPS

JOHN JOUBERT, 1927–
Commissioned for *The Cambridge Hymnal*

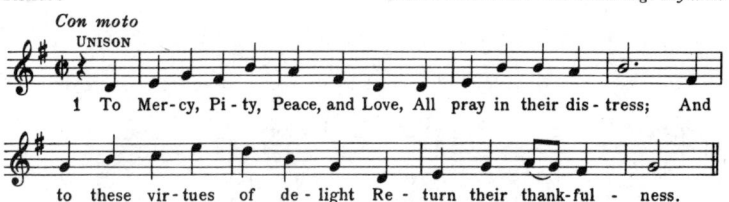

1 To Mercy, Pity, Peace, and Love
  All pray in their distress;
  And to those virtues of delight
  Return their thankfulness.

2 For Mercy, Pity, Peace and Love
  Is God, our father dear,
  And Mercy, Pity, Peace and Love
  Is Man, his child and care.

3 For Mercy has a human heart,
  Pity a human face,
  And love, the human form divine,
  And Peace, the human dress.

4 Then every man of every clime
  That prays in his distress,
  Prays to the human form divine,
  Love, Mercy, Pity, Peace.

5 And all must love the human form,
  In heathen, turk, or jew;
  Where Mercy, Love, and Pity dwell
  There God is dwelling too.

William Blake, 1757–1827

NEWCASTLE — English traditional

1. Up to those bright and gladsome hills,
   Whence flows my weal and mirth,
   I look, and sigh for him who fills,
   Unseen, both heav'n and earth.
   He is alone my help and hope,
   That I shall not be moved;
   His watchful eye is ever ope,
   And guardeth his beloved.

2. The glorious God is my sole stay,
   He is my sun and shade:
   The cold by night, the heat by day,
   Neither shall me invade.
   Whether abroad, amidst the crowd,
   Or else within my door,
   He is my pillar and my cloud,
   Now and for evermore.

Henry Vaughan, 1622–95. From Psalm 121

120

VENI CREATOR (*Plainchant*)

Transcribed by ANTHONY MILNER, 1925–
Commissioned for *The Cambridge Hymnal*

1 Veni, Creator Spiritus,
  Mentes tuorum visita:
  Imple superna gratia
  Quae tu creasti pectora.

2 Qui diceris Paraclitus,
  Altissimi Donum Dei,
  Fons vivus, ignis, caritas,
  Et spiritalis unctio.

3 Tu septiformis munere,
  Digitus Paternae dexterae,
  Tu rite promissum Patris,
  Sermone ditans guttura.

4 Accende lumen sensibus,
  Infunde amorem cordibus,
  Infirma nostri corporis
  Virtute firmans perpeti.

5 Hostem repellas longius,
  Pacemque dones protinus,
  Ductore sic te praevio
  Vitemus omne noxium.

6 Per te sciamus, da, Patrem,
  Noscamus atque Filium,
  Teque utriusque Spiritum
  Credamus omni tempore.

7 Deo Patri sit gloria,
  Et Filio qui a mortuis
  Surrexit, ac Paraclito,
  In saeculorum saecula.

Graduale Monasticum 10*th century or earlier*
Possibly by Rabanus Maurus, 776–856

121

VENI CREATOR

Metrical version by ANTHONY MILNER, 1925-
Commissioned for *The Cambridge Hymnal*

1. Come, Holy Ghost, our souls inspire,
   And lighten with celestial fire;
   Thou the anointing Spirit art,
   Who dost thy sevenfold gifts impart:

2. Thy blessèd unction from above
   Is comfort, life, and fire of love;
   Enable with perpetual light
   The dullness of our blinded sight:

3. Anoint and cheer our soilèd face
   With the abundance of thy grace:
   Keep far our foes, give peace at home;
   Where thou art guide no ill can come.

4. Teach us to know the Father, Son
   And thee, of both, to be but one;
   That through the ages all along
   This may be our endless song:

5. To God the Father glory be,
   To God who died, and rose to thee,
   To God the Paraclete, give praise
   To endless and to endless days.

Bishop J. Cosin, 1594–1672
Based on Veni Creator Spiritus (verse 5, The Cambridge Hymnal, from the Latin)

122

BABYLON'S STREAMS

THOMAS CAMPION, 1575–1619
Transcribed and edited, E. H. Fellowes, 1870–1951

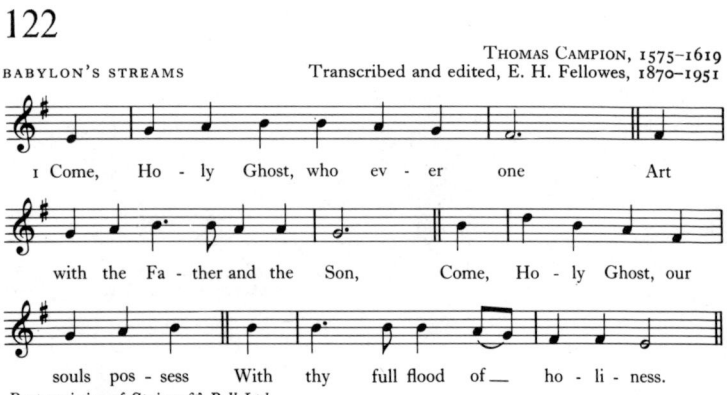

By permission of Stainer & Bell Ltd.

1 Come, Holy Ghost, who ever one
  Art with the Father and the Son,
  Come, Holy Ghost, our souls possess
  With thy full flood of holiness.

2 In will and deed, in heart and tongue,
  With all thy powers, thy praise be sung;
  And love light up our mortal frame
  Till others catch the living flame.

3 Almighty Father, hear our cry
  Through Jesus Christ our Lord most high,
  Who with the Holy Ghost and thee
  Doth live and reign eternally.

St. Ambrose, 340–97
Translated, J. H. Newman, 1801–90

123

JAM LUCIS Plainchant. G. GUIDETTI, *Directorium Chori*, 1582

Come, Holy Ghost, who ev-er one Art with the Fa-ther and the Son,

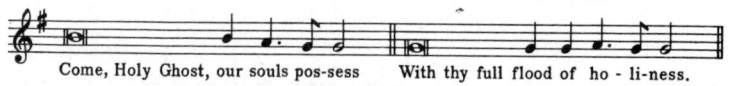

Come, Holy Ghost, our souls pos-sess With thy full flood of ho-li-ness.

1 Come, Holy Ghost, who ever one
  Art with the Father and the Son,
  Come, Holy Ghost, our souls possess
  With thy full flood of holiness.

2 In will and deed, in heart and tongue,
  With all thy powers, thy praise be sung;
  And love light up our mortal frame
  Till others catch the living flame.

3 Almighty Father, hear our cry
  Through Jesus Christ our Lord most high,
  Who with the Holy Ghost and thee
  Doth live and reign eternally.

St. Ambrose, 340–97
Translated, J. H. Newman, 1801–90

124

KOMM, GOTT SCHÖPFER J. S. BACH, 1685–1750

1 Come, Holy Ghost, our souls inspire,
  And lighten with celestial fire;
  Thou the anointing Spirit art,
  Who dost thy sevenfold gifts impart:

Bishop J. Cosin, 1594–1672
Based on Veni Creator Spiritus (verse 5, The Cambridge Hymnal, from the Latin)

125

COLCHESTER

S. S. WESLEY, 1810–76
Descant, E. P.

1. Creator Spirit, by whose aid
   The world's foundations first were laid,
   Come, visit every pious mind;
   Come, pour thy joys on human kind;
   From sin and sorrow set us free,
   And make thy temples worthy thee.

2. O source of uncreated light,
   The Father's promised Paraclete,
   Thrice holy fount, thrice holy fire,
   Our hearts with heavenly love inspire;
   Come, and thy sacred unction bring
   To sanctify us while we sing.

3. Plenteous of grace, descend from high
   Rich in thy sevenfold energy;
   Make us eternal truths receive,
   And practise all that we believe;
   Give us thyself, that we may see
   The Father and the Son by thee.

4. Immortal honour, endless fame,
   Attend the almighty Father's name;
   The saviour Son be glorified,
   Who for lost man's redemption died;
   And equal adoration be,
   Eternal Paraclete, to thee.

J. Dryden, 1631–1700
Based on Veni Creator Spiritus

126

VENI CREATOR

Plainsong melody, Mechlin version
Vesperale Romanum, cum cantu emendato (Mechlin, 1848)

1. Come, Holy Ghost, our souls inspire,
   And lighten with celestial fire;
   Thou the anointing Spirit art,
   Who dost thy sevenfold gifts impart:

2. Thy blessèd unction from above
   Is comfort, life, and fire of love;
   Enable with perpetual light
   The dullness of our blinded sight:

3. Anoint and cheer our soilèd face
   With the abundance of thy grace:
   Keep far our foes, give peace at home;
   Where thou art guide no ill can come.

4. Teach us to know the Father, Son,
   And thee, of Both, to be but One;
   That through the ages all along
   This may be our endless song:
   Praise to thy eternal merit,
   Father, Son, and Holy Spirit. Amen.

Bishop J. Cosin, 1594–1672
Based on Veni Creator Spiritus

127

Thomas Campion, 1567–1620 (composed c. 1613)
Transcribed and edited, E. H. Fellowes, 1870–1951

By Permission of Stainer & Bell Ltd.

1 View me, Lord, a work of thine;
   Shall I then lie drowned in night?
Might thy grace in me but shine,
   I should seem made all of light.

2 But my soul still surfeits so
   On the poisoned baits of sin,
That I strange and ugly grow,
   All is dark and foul within.

3 Cleanse me, Lord, that I may kneel
   At thine altar, pure and white;
They that once thy mercies feel,
   Gaze no more on earth's delight.

4 Worldly joys, like shadows, fade
   When the heavenly light appears;
But the covenants thou hast made,
   Endless, know nor days nor years.

5 In thy word, Lord, is my trust,
   To thy mercies fast I fly.
Though I am but clay and dust,
   Yet thy grace can lift me high.

Thomas Campion, 1567–1620

128

MONKS GATE

Adapted from a traditional Sussex melody
by R. Vaughan Williams, 1872–1958

1. Who would true valour see,
   Let him come hither;
One here will constant be,
   Come wind, come weather.
There's no discouragement
Shall make him once relent
His first avowed intent
   To be a pilgrim.

2 Who so beset him round
   With dismal stories,
Do but themselves confound;
   His strength the more is.
No lion can him fright,
He'll with a giant fight,
But he will have a right
   To be a pilgrim.

3 Hobgoblin nor foul fiend
  Can daunt his spirit:
He knows he at the end
  Shall life inherit.
Then fancies fly away,
He'll fear not what men say,
He'll labour night and day
  To be a pilgrim.

John Bunyan, 1628–88, from 'The Pilgrim's Progress'

129

THOMAS CAMPION, 1567-1620
Transcribed and edited, E. H. FELLOWES, 1870-1951
Descant, E. P.

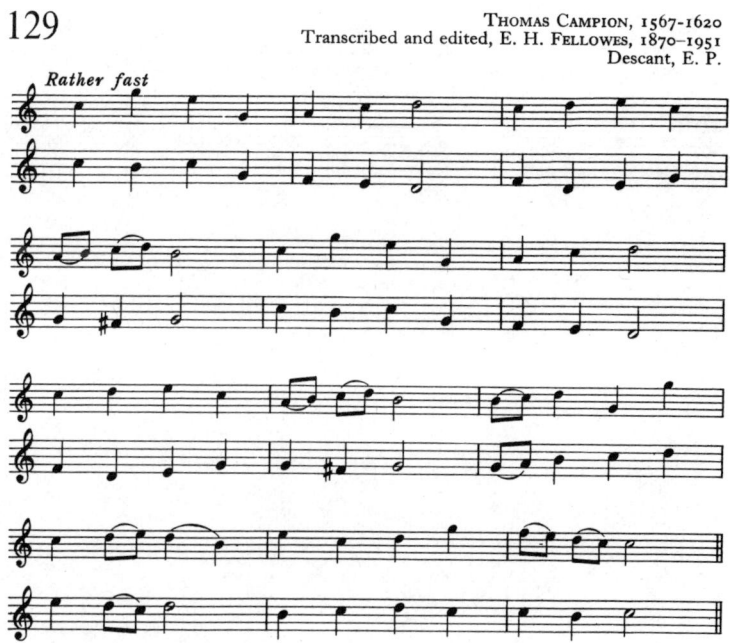

By Permission of Stainer & Bell Ltd.

1 Wise men patience never want,
    Good men pity cannot hide.
  Feeble spirits only vaunt
    Of revenge, the poorest pride.
  He alone forgive that can
  Bears the true soul of a man.

2 Some there are debate that seek,
    Making trouble their content;
  Happy if they wrong the meek,
    Vex them that to peace are bent.
  Such undo the common tie
  Of mankind, society.

3 Deeds from love and words that flow
    Foster like kind April showers;
  In the warm sun all things grow,
    Wholesome fruits and pleasant flowers.
  All so thrives his gentle rays
  Whereon human love displays.

Thomas Campion, 1567–1620

130 A HYMN TO GOD THE FATHER

DONNE

Melody and bass by JOHN HILTON, 1599–1657
Edited, E.P.

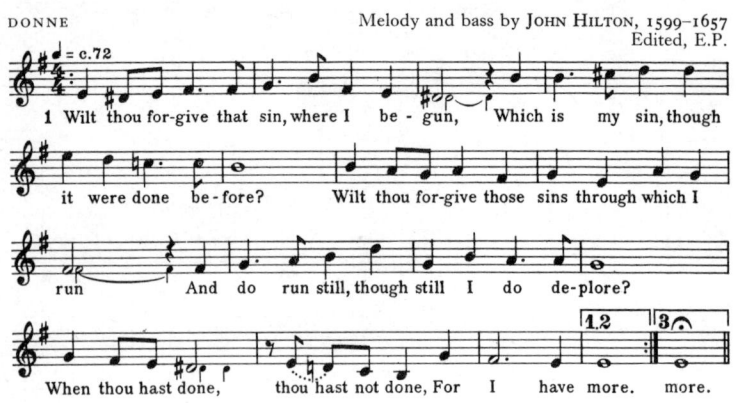

1. Wilt thou forgive that sin, where I begun
   Which is my sin, though it were done before?
   Wilt thou forgive those sins through which I run
   And do run still, though still I do deplore?
   When thou hast done, thou hast not done,
   For I have more.

2. Wilt thou forgive that sin by which I won
   Others to sin? and, made my sin their door?
   Wilt thou forgive that sin which I did shun
   A year or two, but wallowed in, a score?
   When thou hast done, thou hast not done,
   For I have more.

3. I have a sin of fear that when I have spun
   My last thread, I shall perish on the shore;
   Swear by thy self, that at my death thy Son
   Shall shine as he shines now, and heretofore.
   And having done that, thou hast done,
   I fear no more.

John Donne, 1571 or 72–1631

131

PASTHEEN

HAVELOCK NELSON, 1917–
Adapted from an old Irish melody

OUR CHURCH PALMS ARE BUDDING WILLOW TWIGS

While Christ lay dead the widowed world
Wore willow green for hope undone:
Till, when bright Easter dews impearled
The chilly burial earth,
All north and south, all east and west,
Flushed rosy in the arising sun:
Hope laughed, and Faith resumed her rest,
And Love remembered mirth.

Christina Rossetti, 1830–94

132 WERE YOU THERE?

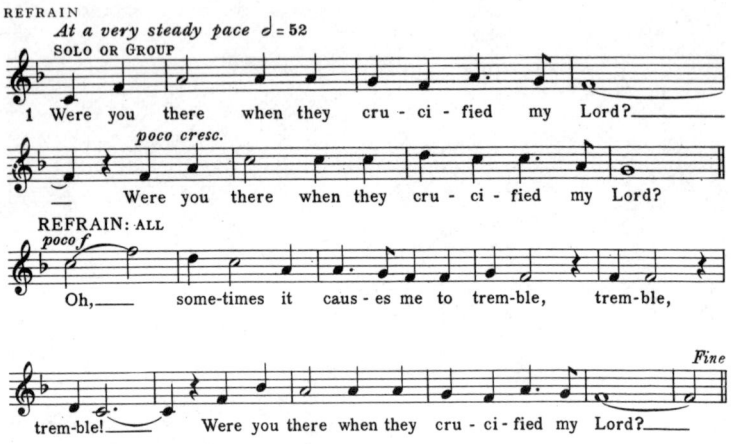

1. Were you there when they crucified my Lord?
   Were you there when they crucified my Lord?
   Oh, sometimes it causes me to tremble!
   Were you there when they crucified my Lord?

2. Were you there when they nailed him to the tree?

3. Were you there when they laid him in the tomb?

4. Were you there when they rolled the stone away?

Negro Spiritual

133

OLD 25TH   Day's *Psalter*, 1565 (rhythm slightly adapted)

In moderate time

1. What creature, O sweet Lord,
   From praising thee can stay?
   What earthly thing, but filled with joy,
   Thine honour doth bewray?
   Let us therefore with praise
   Thy mighty works express,
   With heart and hand, with mind and all
   Which we from thee possess.

2. The roses that appear
   So fair in outward sight,
   The violets which with their scent
   Do yield so great delight;
   The pearls, the precious stones,
   The birds, thy praise do sing;
   The woods, the wells, and all delights
   Which from this earth do spring.

3. The sky, the land, the sea,
   And all on earth below,
   The glory of thy worthy name
   Do with their praises show.
   The winter yields thee praise,
   And summer doth the same;
   The sun, the moon, the stars and all,
   Do magnify thy name.

4. All charity of those
   Whose souls thy love doth warm,
   All simple plainness of such minds
   As think no kind of harm;
   All sweet delights wherewith
   The patient hearts abound,
   Do blaze thy name, and with thy praise
   They make the world resound.

Philip Howard, Earl of Arundel, 1557–95

134

MERCY'S FREE

Primitive American
LEONARD P. BREEDLOVE, 1858
Arranged, E. P.

1 What's this that in my soul is rising?
    Is it grace? Is it grace?
  What's this that in my soul is rising?
    Is it grace? Is it grace?
  This work that's in my soul begun,
  It makes me strive all sin to shun,
  It plants my soul beneath the sun,
    Mercy's free! Mercy's free!

2 Great God of love, I can but wonder,
    Mercy's free! Mercy's free!
  Though I've no price at all to tender,
    Mercy's free! Mercy's free!
  This work that's in my soul begun,
  It makes me strive all sin to shun,
  It plants my soul beneath the sun.
    Mercy's free! Mercy's free!

Leonard P. Breedlove, 1858

135
WONDROUS LOVE

Early American
Arranged, E. P.

1. What wondrous love is this, O my soul, O my soul;
   What wondrous love is this, O my soul;
   What wondrous love is this
   That caused the Lord of bliss
   To bear the dreadful curse for my soul, for my soul,
   To bear the dreadful curse for my soul?

2. When I was sinking down, sinking down, sinking down,
   When I was sinking down, sinking down,
   When I was sinking down
   Beneath God's righteous frown,
   Christ laid aside his crown for my soul, for my soul,
   Christ laid aside his crown for my soul.

3. To God and to the Lamb I will sing, I will sing;
   To God and to the Lamb I will sing;
   To God and to the Lamb
   Who is the great I AM,
   While millions join the theme, I will sing, I will sing,
   While millions join the theme, I will sing.

4. And when from death I'm free, I'll sing on, I'll sing on;
   And when from death I'm free, I'll sing on;
   And when from death I'm free
   I'll sing and joyful be,
   And through eternity I'll sing on, I'll sing on;
   And through eternity I'll sing on.

Anonymous, 1867

136

BELGRAVE

W. HORSLEY, 1774–1858
Descant, JOHN TOOZE, 1918–

In moderate time

1. When all thy mercies, O my God,
   My rising soul surveys,
   Transported with the view, I'm lost
   In wonder, love and praise.

2. Unnumbered comforts to my soul
   Thy tender care bestowed,
   Before my infant heart conceived
   From whom these comforts flowed.

3. When in the slippery paths of youth
   With heedless steps I ran,
   Thine arm unseen conveyed me safe,
   And led me up to man.

4. When worn with sickness oft hast thou
   With health renewed my face;
   And when in sins and sorrows sunk,
   Revived my soul with grace.

5. Through every period of my life
   Thy goodness I'll pursue,
   And after death in distant worlds
   The glorious themè renew.

6. When nature fails, and day and night
   Divide thy works no more
   My ever grateful heart, O Lord,
   Thy mercy shall adore.

7. Through all eternity to thee
   A joyful song I'll raise;
   For O! eternity's too short
   To utter all thy praise.

Joseph Addison, 1672–1719

137

ROCKINGHAM

Revised from the adaptation by E. MILLER, 1790, of an earlier tune
Descant, E. P.

1 With all the powers my poor soul hath
   Of humble love and loyal faith,
 Thus low, my God, I bow to thee,
   Whom too much love bowed lower for me.

2 Down, down, proud sense, discourses die,
   And all adore faith's mystery!
 Faith is my skill, faith can believe
   As fast as love new laws can give.

3 Faith is my force, faith strength affords
   To keep pace with those powerful words:
 And words more sure, more sweet than they,
   Love could not think, truth could not say.

4 O dear memorial of that death,
   Which still survives, and gives us breath,
 Life ever, bread of life, and be
   My food, my joy, my all to me.

5 O soft, self-wounding Pelican!
   Whose breast weeps balm for wounded man,
 That blood, whose least drops sovereign be
   To wash my worlds of sin from me.

6 Come, glorious Lord, my hopes increase,
   And fill my portion in thy peace:
 Come hidden life, and that long day
   For which I languish, come away.

7 When this dry soul those eyes shall see,
   And drink the unsealed source of thee;
 When glory's sun faith's shade shall chase,
   Then for thy veil, give me thy face.

St. Thomas Aquinas, 1227–74
Translated and adapted by K. Crawshaw, 1613–50, and J. Austin, 1613–69

138

DARWALL'S 148TH

J. DARWALL, 1731–89
Descant, W. R. PASFIELD, 1909–

1 Ye holy angels bright,
   Who wait at God's right hand,
 Or through the realms of light
   Fly at your Lord's command,
     Assist our song,
       Or else the theme
       Too high doth seem
     For mortal tongue.

2 Ye blessèd souls at rest
   Who ran this earthly race,
 And now from sin released,
   Behold the Saviour's face,
     His praises sound,
       As in his light
       With sweet delight
     Ye do abound.

3 Ye saints who toil below,
   Adore your heavenly king,
 And onward as ye go
   Some joyful anthem sing:
     Take what he gives,
       And praise him still,
       Through good and ill,
     Who ever lives.

4 My soul, bear thou thy part,
   Triumph in God above,
 And with a well-tuned heart
   Sing thou the songs of love.
     Let all thy days
       Till life shall end,
       What'er he send,
     Be filled with praise.

Richard Baxter, 1615–91, and others

1 The Lord of Heav'n confess;
  On high his glory raise;
  Him let all angels bless,
  Him let all armies praise;
    Him glorify
    Sun, moon, and stars,
    Ye higher spheres,
    And cloudy sky.

2 Praise God from earth below,
  Ye dragons and ye deeps,
  Fire, hail, clouds, winds, and snow,
  Whom in command he keeps;
    Praise ye his name,
    Hills great and small,
    Trees low and tall,
    Beasts wild and tame.

3 O let God's name be praised
  Above both earth and sky;
  For he his saints hath raised,
  And set their horn on high;
    Yea, they that are
    Of Israel's race
    Are in his grace
    And ever dear.

George Wither, 1588–1667. From Psalm 148

139

GRÄFENBERG

Melody in *Praxis Pietatis Melica*, 1653

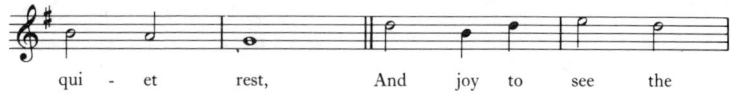
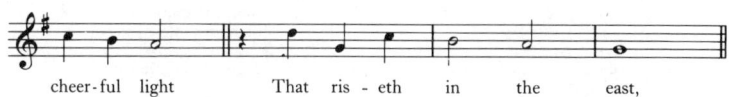

1 You that have spent the silent night
   In sleep and quiet rest,
  And joy to see the cheerful light
   That riseth in the east,

2 Now clear your voice, now cheer your heart,
   Come help me now to sing;
  Each willing wight come bear a part,
   To praise the heavenly King.

3 The little birds which sing so sweet
   Are like the angels' voice,
  Which render God his praises meet,
   And teach us to rejoice.

4 And as they more esteem that mirth
   Than dread the night's annoy,
  So must we deem our days on earth
   But hell to heavenly joy.

5 Unto which joy for to attain
   God grant us all his grace,
  And send us after worldly pain
   In heaven to have a place;

6 Where we may still enjoy that light
   Which never shall decay:
  Lord, for thy mercy lend us might
   To see that joyful day.

George Gascoigne, c. 1525–77

CHRISTMAS HYMNS AND CAROLS

140 DEO GRATIAS

Norman Fulton, 1909–
Commissioned for *The Cambridge Hymnal*

1 Adam lay ybounden,
   Bounden in a bond;
   Four thousand winter
   Thought he not too long.

2 And all was for an apple,
   An apple that he took,
   As clerkès finden
   Written in their book.

3 Ne had the apple taken been,
   The apple taken been,
   Ne had never our lady
   A-been heavenè queen.

4 Blessèd be the time
   That apple taken was.
   Therefore we moun singen
   Deo gratias!

Sloane MS., c. 15th century.

141 (continued)

1. A Virgin most pure, as the prophets do tell,
   Hath brought forth a baby, as it hath befell,
   To be our Redeemer from death, hell, and sin,
   Which Adam's transgression hath wrappèd us in:
   Aye and therefore be merry, rejoice and be you merry,
   Set sorrows aside;
   Christ Jesus our Saviour was born on this tide.

2. At Bethlem in Jewry a city there was,
   Where Joseph and Mary together did pass,
   And there to be taxèd with many one mo',
   For Caesar commanded the same should be so:

3. But when they had entered the city so fair,
   A number of people so mighty was there,
   That Joseph and Mary, whose substance was small,
   Could find in the inn there no lodging at all:

4. Then they were constrained in a stable to lie,
   Where horses and asses they used for to tie;
   Their lodging so simple they took it no scorn,
   But against the next morning our Saviour was born.

5. The King of all kings to this world being brought,
   Small store of fine linen to wrap him was sought;
   And when she had swaddled her young son so sweet,
   Within an ox-manger she laid him to sleep:

6. Then God sent an angel from heaven so high,
   To certain poor shepherds in fields where they lie,
   And bade them no longer in sorrow to stay,
   Because that our Saviour was born on this day:

7. Then presently after the shepherds did spy
   A number of angels that stood in the sky;
   They joyfully talkèd, and sweetly did sing,
   To God be all glory, our heavenly King:

Traditional; this version taken from Davies Gilbert,
'Some Ancient Christmas Carols,' 1822

142   CHANTICLEER'S CAROL

NORMAN FULTON, 1909–
Commissioned for *The Cambridge Hymnal*

1 All this night shrill chanticleer,
  Day's proclaiming trumpeter,
    Claps his wings and loudly cries:
    Mortals, mortals, wake and rise!
      See a wonder
      Heaven is under;
  From the earth is risen a Sun
  Shines all night, though day be done.

2 Wake, O earth, wake everything!
  Wake and hear the joy I bring;
    Wake and joy; for all this night
    Heaven and every twinkling light,
      All amazing,
      Still stand gazing.
  Angels, Powers, and all that be,
  Wake, and joy this Sun to see.

3 Hail, O Sun, O blessèd Light,
  Sent into the world by night!
    Let thy rays and heavenly powers
    Shine in these dark souls of ours;
      For most duly
      Thou art truly
  God and man, we do confess:
  Hail, O Sun of Righteousness!

William Austin of Lincoln's Inn (d. 1633)
From 'A Handfull of Celestial Flowers,' manuscribed by Ralph Crane,
in 'Ancient English Christmas Carols,' Edith Rickert, 1910

143   BEHOLD A SILLY TENDER BABE

Tune from Corner's *Geistliche Gesangbuch*, 1625
Arranged and descant, E.P.

© Elizabeth Poston

1. Behold a silly[1] tender babe
   In freezing winter night
   In homely manger trembling lies;
   Alas a piteous sight.

2. The inns are full, no man will yield
   This little pilgrim bed;
   But forced is he with silly beasts
   In crib to shroud his head.

3. Despise him not for lying there:
   First what he is enquire:
   An orient pearl is often found
   In depth of dirty mire.

4. Weigh not his crib, his wooden dish,
   Nor beasts that by him feed;
   Weigh not his mother's poor attire
   Nor Joseph's simple weed.

5. This stable is a Prince's court,
   The crib his chair of state:
   The beasts are parcel of his pomp,
   The wooden dish his plate.

6. The persons in that poor attire
   His royal liv'ries wear,
   The prince himself is come from heaven,
   This pomp is prized there.

7. With joy approach, O Christian wight,
   Do homage to the King;
   And highly praise his humble pomp
   Which he from heaven doth bring.

Robert Southwell, c. 1561–1595. From 'New Prince, New Pompe'

[1] *silly* = simple, naive, innocent.

144. THE BOAR'S HEAD CAROL

Traditional, Queen's College, Oxford (Brit. Mus. MS. Add. 5665)
Arranged, E. P.

© Elizabeth Poston

1. The boar's head in hand bear I,
   Bedecked with bays and rosemary;
   And I pray you, my masters, be merry,
   Quot estis in convivio:[1]

   Caput apri defero,
   Reddens laudes Domino.[2]

2. The boar's head, as I understand,
   Is the rarest dish in all the land
   When thus bedecked with a gay garland,
   Let us *servire cantico:*[3]

3. Our steward hath provided this
   In honour of the King of bliss,
   Which on this day to be servèd is,
   In Reginensi atrio:[4]

Queen's College, Oxford, version;
first printed in Wynkyn de Worde's 'Christmasse Caroles', 1521

[1] *Quot,* etc. So many as are in the feast.
[2] *Caput,* etc. The boar's head I bring, giving praises to God.
[3] *Servire,* etc. Serve with a song.
[4] *In,* etc. In the Queen's hall.

Words and melody by permission of Stainer & Bell Ltd.

1 Down in yon forest there stands a hall:
   The bells of Paradise I heard them ring:
   It's covered all over with purple and pall:
   And I love my Lord Jesus above anything.

2 In that hall there stands a bed:
   It's covered all over with scarlet so red:

3 At the bed-side there lies a stone:
   Which the sweet Virgin Mary knelt upon:

4 Under that bed there runs a flood:
   The one half runs water, the other runs blood:

5 At the bed's foot there grows a thorn:
   Which ever blows blossom since he was born:

6 Over that bed the moon shines bright:
   Denoting our Saviour was born this night:

Derbyshire Traditional, collected with the music

146 THE FIRST NOWELL

English traditional melody
Descant, E. P.

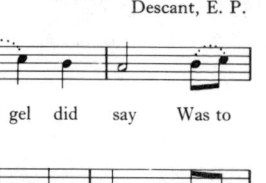
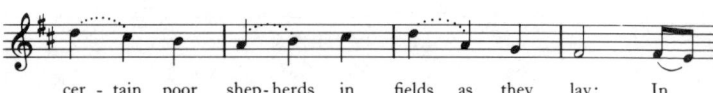

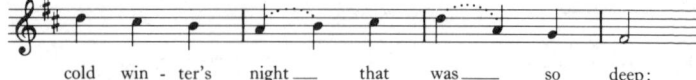

1 The first Nowell the angel did say
   Was to certain poor shepherds in fields as they lay;
   In fields where they lay, keeping their sheep,
   In a cold winter's night that was so deep:

   Nowell, Nowell, Nowell, Nowell,
   Born is the King of Israel!

2 They looked up and saw a star,
   Shining in the east, beyond them far;
   And to the earth it gave great light,
   And it continued both day and night:

3 And by the light of that same star,
   Three Wise Men came from country far;
   To seek for a king was their intent,
   And to follow the star wheresoever it went:

4. This star drew nigh to the north west;
O'er Bethlehem it took its rest,
And there it did both stop and stay
Right over the place where Jesus lay:

5. Then did they know assuredly
Within that house the King did lie:
One entered in then for to see,
And found the babe in poverty:

6. Then entered in those Wise Men three,
Fell reverently upon their knee,
And offered there in his presence
Both gold and myrrh and frankincense:

7. Between an ox-stall and an ass
This child truly there born he was;
For want of clothing they did him lay
All in a manger, among the hay:

8. Then let us all with one accord
Sing praises to our heavenly Lord,
That hath made heaven and earth of nought,
And with his blood mankind hath bought:

9. If we in our time shall do well,
We shall be free from death and hell;
For God hath prepared for us all
A resting place in general:

Traditional, from W. Sandys, 'Christmas Carols Ancient and Modern', 1833

147   FRANCIS KINDLEMARSH'S CAROL

Melody and bass by Orlando Gibbons, 1583–1625
Additional parts and descant by Michael Paget, 1936–
Commissioned for *The Cambridge Hymnal*

SONG 24

Moderately slow

1. From virgin's womb this Christmas day did spring
The precious seed that only savèd man:
This day let man rejoice and sweetly sing
Since on this day salvation first began.
This day did Christ man's soul from death remove,
With glorious saints to dwell in heav'n above.

last line, verse 4 only
DESCANT

The joy of Christ's birth on this day recite.

147 (continued)

1 From virgin's womb this Christmas day did spring
  The precious seed that only savèd man:
This day let man rejoice and sweetly sing
  Since on this day salvation first began.
    This day did Christ man's soul from death remove,
    With glorious saints to dwell in heav'n above.

2 This day to man came pledge of perfect peace:
  This day to man came love and unity:
This day man's grief began for to cease,
  This day did man receive a remedy
    For each offence and ev'ry deadly sin
    That he, with guilty heart, has wandered in.

3 Now in Christ's flock let love be surely placed:
  Now from Christ's flock let concord hate expel:
Now of Christ's flock let love be so embraced,
  As we in Christ, and Christ in us may dwell.
    Christ is the author of all unity,
    From whence proceedeth all felicity.

4 O sing unto this glittering glorious King:
  O praise his name let every living thing:
Let heart and voice like bells of silver ring
  The comfort that this Christmas day did bring.
    Let lute and harp, with sound of sweet delight
    The joy of Christ's birth on this day recite.

'A Carowle for Christmas Day,' by Francis Kindlemarsh (fl. c. 1570),
from 'Songs of Sundry Natures,' by William Byrd (1589)

148   GOD REST YOU MERRY

Traditional English melody, from W. Sandys,
Christmas Carols Ancient and Modern, 1833
Arranged, E. P.

1 God rest you mer-ry, Gen-tle-men, Let no-thing you dis-may, For Je-sus Christ our Sav-iour Was born up-on this day, To save us all from

1 God rest you merry, Gentlemen,
   Let nothing you dismay,
   For Jesus Christ our Saviour
   Was born upon this day,
   To save us all from Satan's power
   When we were gone astray:

   O tidings of comfort and joy.

2 In Bethlehem in Jewry
   This blessèd babe was born,
   And laid within a manger,
   Upon this blessèd morn;
   The which his mother Mary
   Nothing did take in scorn:

3 From God our heavenly Father
   A blessèd angel came,
   And unto certain shepherds
   Brought tidings of the same,
   How that in Bethlehem was born
   The Son of God by name:

4 'Fear not,' then said the angel,
   'Let nothing you affright,
   This day is born a Saviour,
   Of virtue, power, and might;
   So frequently to vanquish all
   The friends of Satan quite:'

5 The shepherds at those tidings
   Rejoicèd much in mind,
   And left their flocks a-feeding,
   In tempest, storm and wind,
   And went to Bethlehem straightway
   This blessèd babe to find:

6 But when to Bethlehem they came,
   Whereat this infant lay,
   They found him in a manger,
   Where oxen feed on hay;
   His mother Mary kneeling,
   Unto the Lord did pray:

7 Now to the Lord sing praises,
   All you within this place,
   And with true love and brotherhood
   Each other now embrace;
   This holy tide of Christmas
   All others doth deface:

   Traditional, from Sandys, 1833

149 HARK, THE HERALD-ANGELS SING

Adapted from a Chorus of FELIX MENDELSSOHN-BARTHOLDY, 1809–47
by W. H. CUMMINGS, 1856

MENDELSSOHN Descant, E. P.

1 Hark, the herald-angels sing 'Glory to the new-born King; Peace on earth, and mercy mild,— God and sinners reconciled!' Joyful, all ye nations, rise,— Join the triumph of the skies;— With the angelic host proclaim 'Christ is born in Bethlehem.' *Hark the herald-angels sing, 'Glory to the new-born King.'*

By permission of Novello & Co. Ltd. ©

1 Hark, the herald-angels sing
 'Glory to the new-born King;
 Peace on earth, and mercy mild,
 God and sinners reconciled!'
 Joyful, all ye nations, rise,
 Join the triumph of the skies;
 With the angelic host proclaim
 'Christ is born in Bethlehem.'

2 Christ, by highest heaven adored,
 Christ, the everlasting Lord,
 Late in time behold him come,
 Offspring of the Virgin's womb.
 Veiled in flesh the Godhead see,
 Hail, the incarnate Deity,
 Pleased as Man with man to dwell,
 Jesus, our Immanuel!

Hark the herald-angels sing,
'Glory to the new-born King.'

3 Hail the heaven-born Prince of Peace!
  Hail, the Sun of Righteousness!
  Light and life to all he brings,
  Risen with healing in his wings;
  Mild he lays his glory by,
  Born that man no more may die,
  Born to raise the sons of earth,
  Born to give them second birth:

*Charles Wesley, 1707–88,
altered by George Whitefield, 1714–70, Martin Madan, 1726–90, and others*

150 THE HOLLY AND THE IVY

English folk carol melody collected, Cecil Sharp
Arranged, BENJAMIN BRITTEN, 1913–

The verses should be sung at a more relaxed tempo than the
refrain. The solos can also be sung by chorus or semi-chorus

By permission of Boosey & Hawkes. ©

1 The holly and the ivy
  Are trees that's both well known;
  Of all the trees that grows in woods,
  The holly bears the crown.

  *The rising of the sun,
  The running of the deer,
  The playing of the merry harp,
  Sweet singing in the choir.*

2 The holly bears a blossom
  As white as any flower;
  And Mary bore sweet Jesus Christ
  To be our sweet Saviour.

3 The holly bears a colour
  As green as any tree;
  And Mary bore sweet Jesus Christ
  To set poor sinners free.

4 The holly bears a berry
  As red as any blood,
  And Mary bore sweet Jesus Christ
  To do poor sinners good.

5 The holly bears a prickle
  As sharp as any thorn;
  And Mary bore sweet Jesus Christ
  At Christmas day in the morn.

6 The holly bears a bark
  As bitter as any gall;
  And Mary bore sweet Jesus Christ
  For to redeem us all.

7 The holly and the ivy
  Are trees that's both well known;
  Of all the trees that grows in woods
  The holly bears the crown.

Traditional (adapted)

151 WATTS'S CRADLE SONG

STANLEY TAYLOR, 1902–
Commissioned for *The Cambridge Hymnal*

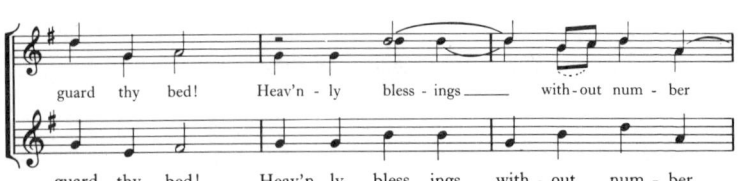

1 Hush! my dear, lie still and slumber;
  Holy Angels guard thy bed!
  Heavenly blessings without number
  Gently falling on thy head.

2 Sleep, my babe; thy food and raiment,
  House and home, thy friends provide;
  All without thy care and payment,
  All thy wants are well supplied.

3 How much better thou'rt attended
  Than the Son of God could be
  When from Heaven he descended
  And became a child like thee.

4 Soft and easy is thy cradle;
  Coarse and hard thy Saviour lay,
  When his birthplace was a stable
  And his softest bed was hay.

5 Lo, he slumbers in his manger,
  Where the hornèd oxen fed;
  Peace, my darling! here's no danger;
  Here's no ox a-near thy bed.

6 Mayst thou live to know and fear him,
  Trust and love him all thy days:
  Then go dwell for ever near him,
  See his face and sing his praise.

Isaac Watts, 1674–1748

152 I SING OF A MAIDEN

LENNOX BERKELEY, 1903–
Commissioned for *The Cambridge Hymnal*

1 I sing of a maiden
   That is makèless,[1]
   King of all kingès
   To her son she ches.[2]

2 He came all so stillè
   There his mother was,
   As dew in Aprillè
   That falleth on the grass.

3 He came all so stillè
   To his mother's bowr,
   As dew in Aprillè
   That falleth on the flowr.

4 He came all so stillè
   There his mother lay,
   As dew in Aprillè
   That falleth on the spray.

5 Mother and maiden
   Was never none but she;
   Well may such a lady
   Godès mother be.

15*th century, from Sloane MS.*, 2593, *as in* 'Early English Lyrics,'
E. K. Chambers *and* F. Sidgwick, 1947.

[1] *makeless* = matchless.
[2] *ches* = chose.

153   IN A FIELD AS I LAY
SOLO SA/UNISON ACCOMPANIED OR
SOLI AND 4-PART CHORUS

CHRISTOPHER MORRIS, 1922–
Commissioned for *The Cambridge Hymnal*

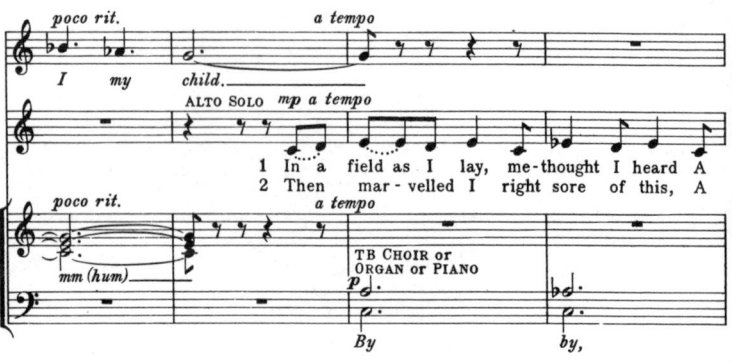

By by, lullaby,
Rocked I my child.

1 In a field as I lay, methought I heard
   A maiden say and speak these wordés wild:
   My little son, with thee I play and sing;
   Thus rocked she her child:

2 Then marvelled I right sore of this,
   A maid to have a child, ewis;
   My sweetest son, and yet my King of bliss;
   Thus rocked she her child:

14th century (altered)

154
CRANHAM

GUSTAV HOLST, 1874–1934

By kind permission of Miss Imogen Holst and the Trustees of the late Gustav Holst.

1 In the bleak mid-winter
   Frosty wind made moan,
Earth stood hard as iron,
   Water like a stone;
Snow had fallen, snow on snow,
   Snow on snow,
In the bleak mid-winter,
   Long ago.

2 Our God, heaven cannot hold him
   Nor earth sustain;
Heaven and earth shall flee away
   When he comes to reign:
In the bleak mid-winter
   A stable-place sufficed
The Lord God almighty,
   Jesus Christ.

3 Enough for him, whom cherubim
    Worship night and day,
  A breastful of milk
    And a mangerful of hay;
  Enough for him, whom angels
    Fall down before,
  The ox and ass and camel
    Which adore.

4 What can I give him,
    Poor as I am?
  If I were a shepherd
    I would bring a lamb;
  If I were a wise man
    I would do my part;
  Yet what I can I give him –
    Give my heart.

Christina Rossetti, 1830–94

155 POOR LITTLE JESUS

American traditional
Arranged, E. P.

1 It was poor little Jesus, Yes, yes; He was born on Christmas, Yes, yes; And laid in a manger, Yes, yes; Wasn't that a pity and a shame, Lord, Lord,

4 It was poor little Jesus, Yes, yes; He's risen from darkness, Yes, yes; 'scended into glory, Yes, yes; No more a pity and a shame, Lord, Lord,

DESCANT (*last verse only*): He's 'scended into glory, glory, No more a pity and a shame, Lord, Lord,

155 (continued)

[Music: last time f, Fine]

No more a pi-ty and a shame.

Was-n't that a pi-ty and a shame?
No more a pi-ty and a shame.

GROUP
2 It was poor lit-tle Je-sus,
3 It was poor lit-tle Je-sus,

CHORUS
Yes, yes;
Verse 2 only

(v.2) — **GROUP**
Child of Ma-ry,
They nailed him to the cross, Lord,

CHORUS
Yes, yes;

GROUP
Did-n't have no cra-dle,
They hung him with a rob-ber,

CHORUS
Yes, yes;

Was-n't that a pi-ty and a shame, Lord, Lord,

2nd time D.S. (v.4)

Was-n't that a pi-ty and a shame?

1 It was poor little Jesus,
    Yes, yes;
He was born on Christmas,
    Yes, yes;
And laid in a manger,
    Yes, yes;
  Wasn't that a pity and a shame,
    Lord, Lord,
  Wasn't that a pity and a shame?

2 It was poor little Jesus,
  Child of Mary,
  Didn't have no cradle,

3 It was poor little Jesus,
  They nailed him to the cross, Lord,
  They hung him with a robber,

4 It was poor little Jesus,
  He's risen from darkness,
  He's 'scended into glory,
    No more a pity and a shame.

American traditional (slightly adapted).
Collected from coloured children in New York State and
printed in W. W. Newell, 'Songs and Games of American Children,' 1884–1911

156 WHERE RICHES IS EVERLASTINGLY
(Into this world this day did come)

PETER WARLOCK, 1894–1930

1 Into this world this day did come
  Jesus Christ, both God and man,
  Lord and Servant in one person,
  Born of the blessed Virgin Mary.
  *I pray you be merry and sing with me
  In worship of Christ's nativity.*

2 He that was rich without any need
  Appear'd in this world in right poor weed
  To make us, that were poor indeed,
  Rich without any need truly.

3 A stable was his chamber, a cratch[1] was his bed,
  He had not a pillow to lay under his head;
  With maiden's milk that Babe was fed,
  In poor clothes was lapped the Lord Almighty.

4 A noble lesson here is us taught,
  To set all worldly riches at naught,
  But pray we that we may be thither brought
  Where riches is everlastingly.

[1] *cratch* = crèche, crib or manger.

16th century. Balliol College, Oxford, MS. 354

* Verse 3 may be sung as a solo, with harmonized chorus ad lib.

Copyright in U.S.A. and all countries, 1928, by the Oxford University Press, London

157

WHITLAND

WILLIAM MATHIAS, 1924–
Commissioned for *The Cambridge Hymnal*

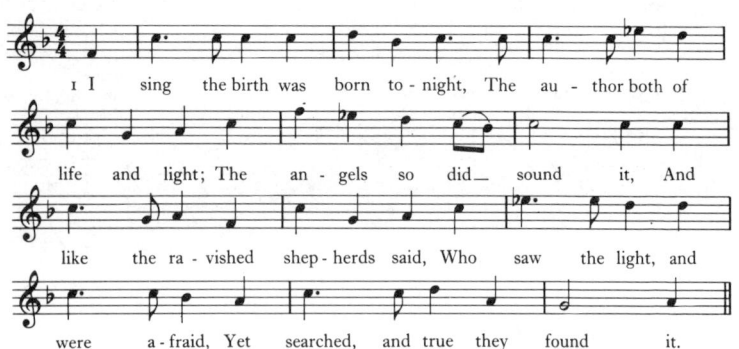

1. I sing the birth was born tonight,
   The author both of life and light;
   The angels so did sound it,
   And like the ravished shepherds said,
   Who saw the light, and were afraid,
   Yet searched, and true they found it.

2. The Son of God, th' Eternal King,
   That did us all salvation bring,
   And freed the soul from danger;
   He whom the whole world could not take,
   The Word, which heaven and earth did make,
   Was now laid in a manger.

3. The Father's wisdom willed it so,
   The Son's obedience knew no No,
   Both wills were in one stature;
   And as that wisdom had decreed,
   The Word was now made flesh indeed,
   And took on Him our nature.

4. What comfort by him do we win?
   Who made himself the price of sin,
   To make us heirs of glory!
   To see this Babe, all innocence,
   A martyr born in our defence –
   Can man forget this story?

Ben Jonson, 1572–1637

158 JESUS BORN IN BETH'NY

Traditional melody from Virginia
Collected, John Jacob Niles, arranged E. P.

Je - sus born in Beth' - ny, and in a man - ger lay.

By permission of G. Schirmer Inc., New York.
(Chappell & Co. Ltd., London).

1. Jesus born in Beth'ny, Jesus born in Beth'ny,
   Jesus born in Beth'ny, and in a manger lay;
   In a manger lay, in a manger lay,
   Jesus born in Beth'ny, and in a manger lay.

2. Jesus went a-preachin', Jesus went a-preachin',
   Jesus went a-preachin' the Gospel of his God;
   Gospel of his Father, Gospel of his God,
   Jesus went a-preachin' the Gospel of his God.

3. Judas did betray him, Judas did betray him,
   Judas did betray him and sold him for a bribe;
   Sold him for a bribe, sold him for a bribe.
   Judas did betray him and sold him for a bribe.

4. They did crucify him, they did crucify him,
   They did crucify him and nailed him to the tree;
   Nailed him to the tree, nailed him to the tree,
   They did crucify him and nailed him to the tree.

5. Joseph begged his body, Joseph begged his body,
   Joseph begged his body and placed it in a tomb;
   Placed it in a tomb, placed it in a tomb,
   Joseph begged his body and placed it in a tomb.

6. Tomb it would not hold him, tomb it would not hold him,
   Tomb it would not hold him, it burst the bonds of death;
   Burst the bonds of death, burst the bonds of death,
   Tomb it would not hold him, it burst the bonds of death.

7. Early then one morning, early then one morning,
   Early then one morning, before the break of day,
   Came a heavenly angel, rolled the stone away,
   Early then one morning, before the break of day.

8. Mary came a-weeping, Mary came a-weeping,
   Mary came a-weeping, 'They've stole my Lord away;
   Stole my Lord away, stole my Lord away.'
   Mary came a-weeping, 'They've stole my Lord away.'

9. Jesus has arisen, Jesus has arisen,
   Jesus has arisen, and gone to Galilee;
   Gone to Galilee, gone to Galilee,
   Jesus has arisen and gone to Galilee.

10. Jesus then ascended, Jesus then ascended,
    Jesus then ascended up to his Father's throne;
    To his Father's throne, to his Father's throne,
    Jesus then ascended up to his Father's throne.

Traditional, Virginia
Verses 3 and 4 modified in this edition.

159 CHRISTMAS DAY

ELIZABETH POSTON, 1905–

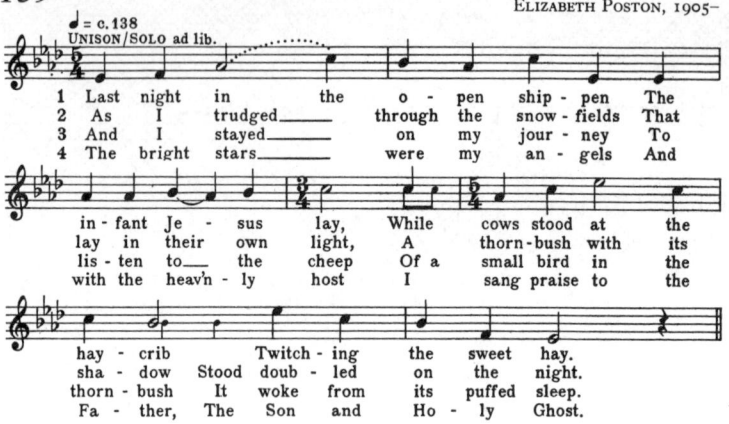

1 Last night in the open shippen[1]
  The infant Jesus lay,
  While cows stood at the hay-crib
  Twitching the sweet hay.

2 As I trudged through the snow-fields
  That lay in their own light,
  A thorn bush with its shadow
  Stood doubled on the night.

[1] *shippen* = cattle-shed.

3 And I stayed on my journey
  To listen to the cheep
  Of a small bird in the thorn-bush
  It woke from its puffed sleep

4 The bright stars were my angels
  And with the heavenly host
  I sang praise to the Father,
  The Son and Holy Ghost.

Andrew Young, 1885–1971

160 LULLAY, LULLAY, THOU LYTIL CHILD

ALAN RIDOUT, 1934–
Commissioned for *The Cambridge Hymnal*

1 Lullay, lullay, thou lytil child,
  Sleep and be well still;
  The King of bliss thy father is,
  As it was his will.

2 This other night I saw a sight,
  A maid a cradle keep:
  'Lullay,' she sung, and said among,
  'Lie still, my child, and sleep.'

3 'How should I sleep? I may not for weep,
   So sore I am begone:
   Sleep I would; I may not for cold,
   And clothes have I none.

4 'For Adam's guilt mankind is spilt
   And that me rueth sore;
   For Adam and Eve here shall I live
   Thirty winter and more.'

'Early English Carols,' ed. R. L. Greene
15th century. From a MS. in Cambridge University Library. (Add. 5943)

161 LULLAY MY LIKING

Gustav Holst, 1874–1934

Lul - lay my lik - ing, my dear son, my sweet - ing;
Lul - lay my dear heart, mine own dear dar - ling!

1 I saw a fair maid - en Sit - ten and sing: She
lul - ted a lit - tle child, A sweet - è loud - ing:

2 That e - ter - nal lord is he That made al - lè thing; Of
al - lè lord - es he is Lord, Of al - lè king - ès King:

3 There was mic - kle mel - o - dy At that child - ès birth: Al - though
they were in hea - ven's bliss They ma - dè mic - kle mirth:

4 An - gels bright they sang that night And said - en to that child:

161 (continued)

'Bless-ed be thou, and so be she That is both meek and mild:'

5 Pray we now to that child, And to his moth-er dear, God grant them all his bless-ing That now mak-en cheer:

Copyright, 1919, by J. Curwen & Sons Ltd.
By permission, from Curwen Edition No. 80589, published by J. Curwen & Sons Ltd., London.

Lullay my liking, my
dear son, my sweeting;
Lullay my dear heart, mine
own dear darling!

1 I saw a fair maiden
Sitten and sing:
She lullèd a little child,
A sweetè lording:

2 That eternal lord is he
That made allè thing;
Of allè lordès he is Lord,
Of allè kingès King:

3 There was a mickle melody
At that childès birth:
Although they were in heaven's bliss
They madè mickle mirth:

4 Angels bright they sang that night
And saiden to that child:
'Blessed be thou, and so be she
That is both meek and mild':

5 Pray we now to that child,
And to his mother dear,
God grant them all his blessing
That now maken cheer:

Sloane MS. 15th century

162 NOWELL, NOWELL, NOWELL

3-part unacc. (S.A.T. and/or B)

ELIZABETH MACONCHY, 1907–
Commissioned for *The Cambridge Hymnal*

162 (continued)

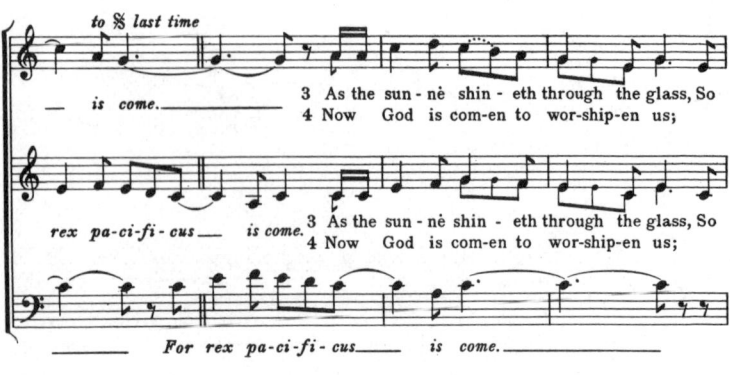

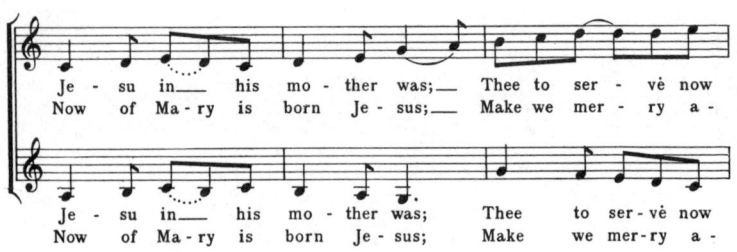

*Nowell, Nowell, Nowell
sing we now all and some,
For rex pacificus[1] is come.*

1 In Bethlehem in that fair city,
   A child was born of a maiden free;
   That shall a lord and princè be;
   A solis ortus cardine.[2]

2 Children were slain in full great plenty,
   Jesus, for the love of thee;
   Wherefore their soulès savèd be;
   Hostis Herodis impie.[3]

3 As the sunnè shineth through the glass,
   So Jesu in his mother was;
   Thee to servè now grant us grace;
   O lux beata Trinitas.[4]

4 Now God is comen to worshipen[5] us;
   Now of Mary is born Jesus;
   Make we merry amongès us;
   Exultet coelum laudibus.[6]

*Trinity College, Cambridge, MS. 0.3.58, late 15th century
From a collection of English songs and hymns, by James Ryman, a Franciscan friar.
Printed in 'Musica Britannica,' ed. J. Stevens, 1958*

[1] The King of peace.
[2] From the rising point of the sun.
[3] Herod, ungodly enemy.
[4] O Light, blessed Trinity.
[5] *worshipen* = bless.
[6] Let the sky exult with praises.

163 BALULALOW
(O My Deir Heart)

Traditional Scots
Arranged, E. P.

© Elizabeth Poston

1 O my deir heart, young Jesus sweet,
  Prepare thy cradle in my spreit;
  And I sall rock thee in my heart,
  And nevermair from thee depart.

2 But I sall praise thee evermore
  With sangès sweet unto thy gloir;
  The knees of my heart sall I bow,
  And sing that richt *Balulalow!*

T. Wedderburn, 1567
From 'Ane Sang of the Birth of Christ,'
from 'Ane Compendious Buik of Godly and Spirituell Sangis,' 1567,
by *James Wedderburn* (1495?–1553), *John Wedderburn* (1500?–1556),
and *Robert Wedderburn* (1510?–1557?). The poem is a translation of a
Christmas carol by Martin Luther (1483–1546), from 'Geistliche Lieder' (1535)

164
ADESTE FIDELES

Music in the MS. of J. F. Wade, 1711–86
Descant, E. P.

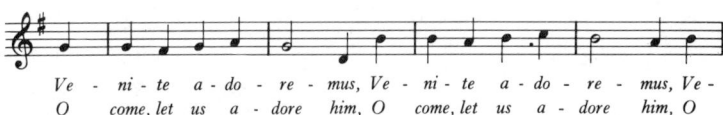

164 (continued)

1. Adeste fideles,
   Laeti triumphantes,
   Venite, venite in Bethlehem;
   Natum videte
   Regem angelorum:

   Venite adoremus,
   Venite adoremus,
   Venite adoremus Dominum.

2. Deum de Deo,
   Lumen de Lumine,
   Gestant puellae viscera;
   Deum verum
   Genitum non factum:

3. Cantet nunc io
   Chorus angelorum,
   Cantet nunc aula caelestium;
   Gloria
   In excelsis Deo:

4. Ergo qui natus
   Die hodierna,
   Jesu tibi sit gloria;
   Patris aeterni
   Verbum caro factum:

1. O come, all ye faithful,
   Joyful and triumphant,
   O come ye, O come ye to Bethlehem;
   Come and behold him,
   Born the King of angels:

   O come, let us adore him,
   O come, let us adore him,
   O come, let us adore him, Christ the Lord.

2. God of God,
   Light of Light,
   Lo, he abhors not the Virgin's womb;
   Very God,
   Begotten, not created:

3. Sing, choirs of angels,
   Sing in exultation,
   Sing, all ye citizens of heaven above;
   Glory to God
   In the highest:

4. Yea, Lord, we greet thee,
   Born this happy morning,
   Jesu, to thee be glory given;
   Word of the Father,
   Now in flesh appearing:

Hymn on the Prose for Christmas Day, ascribed to J. F. Wade, 1711–86

165

Sussex traditional, collected and arranged, R. Vaughan Williams (1872–1956)
Adapted, E. Harold Geer

By permission of Stainer & Bell Ltd.

1 On Christmas night all Christians sing,
To hear the news the angels bring;
News of great joy, news of great mirth,
News of our merciful King's birth.

2 Then why should men on earth be so sad,
Since our Redeemer made us glad,
When from our sin he set us free,
All for to gain our liberty.

3 When sin departs before his grace,
Then life and health come in its place;
Angels and men with joy may sing,
All for to see the new-born King.

4 All out of darkness we have light,
Which made the angels sing this night:
'Glory to God and peace to men,
Now and for evermore. Amen.'

Traditional

QUI CREAVIT COELUM

Lydian with metrical rhythm
Harmonized by ANTHONY MILNER, 1925–
Commissioned for *The Cambridge Hymnal*

Lydian with free rhythm
Harmonized by ANTHONY MILNER

1 Qui creavit coelum,[1]
   Lully, lully, lu,
   Nascitur in stabulo,[2]
   By, by, by, by, by,
   Rex qui regit seculum,[3]
   Lully, lully, lu.

2 Joseph emit panniculum,[4]
   Lully, lully, lu,
   Mater involvit puerum,[5]
   By, by, by, by, by,
   Et ponit in presepio,[6]
   Lully, lully, lu.

3 Inter animalia,[7]
   Lully, lully, lu,
   Jacent mundi gaudia,[8]
   By, by, by, by, by,
   Dulcis super omnia,[9]
   Lully, lully, lu.

4 Lactat mater domini,[10]
   Lully, lully, lu,
   Osculatur parvulum,[11]
   By, by, by, by, by,
   Et adorat dominum,[12]
   Lully, lully, lu.

[1] He who created the heavens
[2] Is born in a stable
[3] The King who rules the ages
[4] Joseph buys a little shawl
[5] Mary swaddles her child
[6] And puts him in a manger
[7] Among the animals
[8] Lie the joys of the world
[9] Sweet above all things
[10] The mother of the Lord feeds him
[11] She kisses the little one
[12] And adores her lord

5 Roga mater filium,[13]
  Lully, lully, lu,
  Ut det nobis gaudium,[14]
  By, by, by, by, by,
  In perenni gloria,[15]
  Lully, lully, lu.

6 In sempiterna secula,[16]
  Lully, lully, lu,
  In eternum et ultra,[17]
  By, by, by, by, by,
  Det nobis sua gaudia,[18]
  Lully, lully, lu,
  (Spoken) Puer natus est nobis![19]

*Chester MS., c. 1425. 'The Processional of the Nuns of Chester,'
ed. J. Wickham Legg, 1899, for the Henry Bradshaw Society (No. XVIII)*

[13] Mother pray your son
[14] That he shall give us bliss
[15] Glory (to him) for ever
[16] World without end
[17] For ever and ever
[18] May he give us his joys
[19] Unto us a son is born

167 SING, ALL MEN

Kentucky Folk Carol, collected John Jacob Niles
Arranged, E. P.

1 Sing, all men! 'tis Christ-mas morn-ing, Je-sus Christ the Son's a-born-ing.
2 Come ye brave, and come ye strong, Re-pent your sins, give up the wrong.
  } Heigh, the hol-ly! Ho, the heath-er! Ca-rol voic-es all to-geth-er!

p 3 In the man-ger all a-lone, The vir-gin moth-er did a-tone.
mp 4 Seek not earth-ly pow'r and pelf, But thro' your Je-sus save your-self.
  } Heigh, the hol-ly! Ho, the heath-er! Ca-rol voic-es all to-geth-er!

mp 5 See the ox and see the kine, And see a-far the heav'n-ly sign.
p 6 He who came on earth so low, Soon to man's e-state will grow.

Heigh, the hol-ly! Ho, the heath-er! Ca-rol voic-es all to-geth-er!

167 (continued)

By permission of G. Schirmer Inc., New York
(Chappell & Co. Ltd., London)

1. Sing, all men! 'tis Christmas morning,
   Jesus Christ the Son's a-borning.

   Heigh, the holly! Ho, the heather!
   Carol voices all together!

2. Come ye brave, and come ye strong,
   Repent your sins, give up the wrong

3. In the manger all alone,
   The virgin mother did atone.

4. Seek not earthly power and pelf,
   But thro' your Jesus save yourself.

5. See the ox and see the kine,
   And see afar the heavenly sign.

6. He who came on earth so low,
   Soon to man's estate will grow.

7. And upon the cruel tree,
   Will die in place of you and me.

Kentucky, traditional

168 SWEET WAS THE SONG
(Virgin's Lullaby)

STANLEY TAYLOR, 1902–72
This arrangement commissioned for *The Cambridge Hymnal*

Andante con moto e legatissimo ♪ = 132
Gently—following the rise and fall of phrase

OPTIONAL ALTOS: Lulla, lulla, lulla, lulla,

SOPRANOS *p dolce*: Sweet was the song the Virgin sung, When she to Bethlem Juda came, And was delivered of a Son, That blessèd Jesus hath to name.

Lullaby; lullaby, lullaby, lullaby.

mp un poco ritmico Lulla, lulla, lulla, lullaby,

Lulla, lulla, lulla, lullaby, sweet Babe, sang she. My

UNIS. *mf* lulla-by, la-lu-la, lulla-

155

168 (continued)

By courtesy of J. Curwen & Sons Ltd.

Sweet was the song the Virgin sung,
When she to Bethlem Juda came,
And was delivered of a Son,
That blessèd Jesus hath to name.
'Lulla, lulla, lulla, lullaby, sweet Babe,' sang she,
'My Son and eke a Saviour born,
Who hast vouchsafèd from on high
To visit us that were forlorn.'
'Lalula, lalula, lalulaby, sweet Babe,' sang she,
And rocked Him sweetly on her knee.

From William Ballet's Lute Book, 17th century;
MS. in Trinity College, Dublin

169 THAT LORD THAT LAY IN ASSĖ STALL

IMOGEN HOLST, 1907–
Commissioned for *The Cambridge Hymnal*

1 That Lord that lay in as-sè stall, Came to die for us all, To make us free that erst were thrall,—

4 Now bless-èd be this Lord be-nign, That nold his cru-el death re-sign, But for mankind to die un-dign,—

REFRAIN
Qui na-tus fu-it ho-di-e, Qui na-tus fu-it ho-di-e, ho-di-e. *Fine*

2 Well may we glad and mer-ry be, Since we were thrall and now be free; The fiend our foe he made to flee, Qui na-tus fu-it ho-di-e. *repeat* REFRAIN

169 (continued)

1. That Lord that lay in assè stall,
   Came to die for us all,
   To make us free that erst were thrall,
   Qui natus fuit hodie.[1]

2. Well may we glad and merry be,
   Since we were thrall and now be free;
   The fiend our foe he made to flee,
   Qui natus fuit hodie.

3. And since our foe is fled from us,
   We may well sing and say right thus:
   'Welcome he be, this Lord Jesus,
   Qui natus fuit hodie.'

4. Now blessèd be this Lord benign,
   That nold[2] his cruel death resign,
   But for mankind to die undign,[3]
   Qui natus fuit hodie.

[1] Who was born today
[2] *nold* = would not
[3] *undign* = unworthy

15th century. Bodleian Library MS. Arch. Selden B 26, printed in 'Lyrics of the Fifteenth Century,' Carleton Brain, p. 118.

170 COVERDALE'S CAROL

R. Vaughan Williams, 1872–1958 (in *Hodie*)

Andante sostenuto ♩ = 100
p, dolce

1 The bless-ed son of God only In a crib full

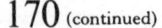

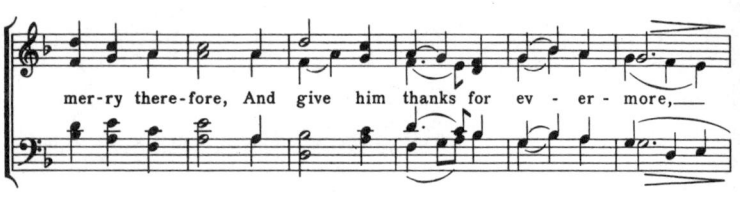

© *Oxford University Press*

1. The blessed son of God only
   In a crib full poor did lie;
   With our poor flesh and our poor blood
   Was clothed that everlasting good.
   Kyrieleison.

2. The Lord Christ Jesu, God's son dear,
   Was a guest and a stranger here;
   Us for to bring from misery,
   That we might live eternally.
   Kyrieleison.

3. All this he did for us freely,
   For to declare his great mercy;
   All Christendom be merry therefore,
   And give him thanks for evermore.
   Kyrieleison.

Miles Coverdale (1487–1568) after Martin Luther

171. THE VIRGIN MARY HAD A BABY BOY

West Indian traditional carol
Collected, EDRIC CONNOR
Arranged, E. P.

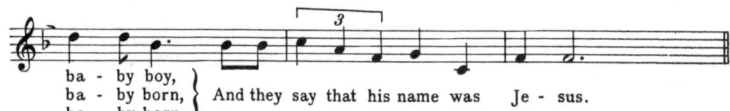

1. The Virgin Mary had a baby boy,
2. The angels sang when the baby born,
3. The wise men saw when the baby born,

The Virgin Mary had a baby boy,
The angels sang when the baby born,
The wise men saw where the baby born,

The Virgin Mary had a baby boy,
The angels sang when the baby born,
The wise men went where the baby born,
And they say that his name was Jesus.

He come from the glory, He come from the glorious kingdom.

Oh, yes! Believer; Oh, yes! Believer;

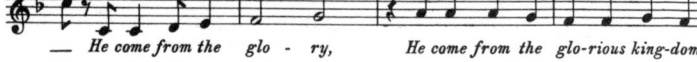

He come from the glory, He come from the glorious kingdom.

THE VIRGIN MARY HAD A BABY BOY

1 The Virgin Mary had a baby boy,[1]
The Virgin Mary had a baby boy,
The Virgin Mary had a baby boy,
And they say that his name was Jesus.

He come from the glory,
He come from the glorious kingdom;
He come from the glory,
He come from the glorious kingdom;

Oh, yes! Believer;
Oh, yes! Believer;
He come from the glory,
He come from the glorious kingdom.

2 The angels sang when the baby born,[2]
And proclaim him the Saviour Jesus.

3 The wise men saw when the baby born,
The wise men saw where the baby born,
The wise men went where the baby born,
And they say that his name was Jesus.

West Indian traditional, collected by Edric Connor

[1] In the original 'De Virgin Mary'.
[2] In the original, 'De baby born'.
Taken down from the singing of the Negro James Bryce in 1942 when Bryce was 92 years old.

Words and melody reprinted from the Edric Connor Collection of West Indian Spirituals and Folk Tunes by permission of Boosey & Hawkes Music Publishers Ltd.

172 THERE IS NO ROSE OF SUCH VIRTUE

Anonymous, *c.* 1420
Transcribed and edited by John Stevens

Printed by permission of the Royal Musical Association

The melody lines of this carol are apt for voice and instrument and are interchangeable; the lower melody and its adjoining part may also be sung an octave higher in the treble clef. An optional 'mean' or middle part, added by the editor, is printed in small notes.

There is no rose of such virtue,
As is the rose that bare Jesu.

1 There is no rose of such virtue
  As is the rose that bare Jesu;
  Alleluia.

2 For in this rose containèd was
  Heaven and earth in little space;
  Res miranda.[1]

3 By that rose we may well see
  That he is God in persons three,
  Pari forma.[2]

4 The angels sungen the shepherds to:
  Gloria in excelsis Deo:
  Gaudeamus.[3]

5 Leave we all this worldly mirth,
  And follow we this joyful birth;
  Transeamus.[4]

15th century.   Trinity College, Cambridge, MS. o.3.58

[1] Marvellous thing
[2] Of equal form
[3] Let us rejoice
[4] Let us go across (from worldly to heavenly things)

173 THERE IS NO ROSE OF SUCH VIRTUE

Anonymous, c. 1420
Transcribed and edited by John Stevens

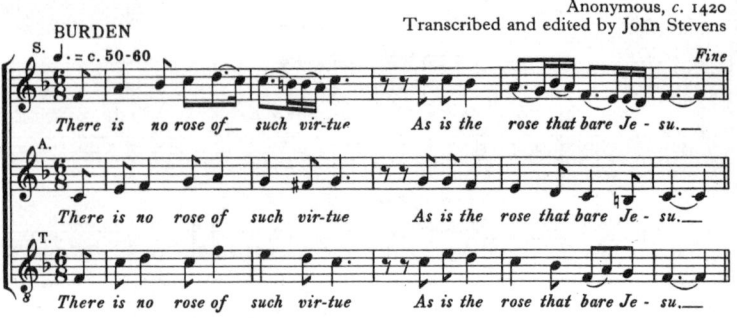

© Copyright 1963 by Stainer & Bell Ltd. Printed by permission

Note by John Stevens:

From a MS. roll of carols, copied out in the early 15th century and now in the Library of Trinity College, Cambridge; printed by kind permission. The carol begins and ends with the chorus (the alto part is editorial and may be omitted at will); the verses are for soloists. Small accidentals in the chorus are absent from the MS. and may be ignored if you wish. The tenor has the tune throughout, and the other voices should be subordinate. The music was intended to be sung unaccompanied.

174 THIS ENDRIS NIGHT

English carol melody, 15th–16th century
Arranged, E. P.

© Elizabeth Poston

1   This endris night[1]
    I saw a sight,
    A star as bright as day;
    And ever among,[2]
    A maiden sung,
    'Lullay, by, by, lullay.'

2   This lovely lady sat and sung,
    And to her child did say:
    'My son, my brother, father, dear,
    Why liest thou thus in hay?
    My sweetest bird, thus 'tis required,
    Though thou be king veray;[3]
    But nevertheless I will not cease
    To sing, By, by, lullay.'

3   The child then spake in his talking,
    And to his mother said:
    'Yea, I am known as heaven-king,
    In crib though I be laid;
    For angels bright down to me light:[4]
    Thou knowest 'tis no nay:[5]
    And for that sight thou may'st delight
    To sing, By, by, lullay.'

4   'Now sweet son, since thou art a king,
    Why art thou laid in stall?
    Why dost not order thy bedding
    In some great kinges hall?
    Methinks 'tis right that king or knight
    Should lie in good array:
    And then among, it were no wrong
    To sing, By, by, lullay.'

5   'Mary mother, I am thy child,
    Though I be laid in stall;
    For lords and dukes shall worship me,
    And so shall kingès all.
    Ye shall well see that Kingès three
    Shall come on this twelfth day,
    For this behest give me thy breast,
    And sing, By, by, lullay.'

6   'Now tell, sweet son, I thee do pray
    Thou art my love and dear –
    How should I keep thee to thy pay,[6]
    And make thee glad of cheer?
    For all thy will I would fulfil –
    Thou knowest well, in fay;[7]
    And for all this I will thee kiss,
    And sing, By, by, lullay.'

7   'My dear mother, when time it be,
    Take thou me up on loft,
    And set me then upon thy knee,
    And handle me full soft;
    And in thy arm thou hold me warm,
    And keep me night and day,
    And if I weep, and may not sleep,
    Thou sing, by, by, lullay.'

8   'Now sweet son, since it is come so,
    That all is at thy will,
    I pray thee grant to me a boon,
    If it be right and skill,[8] –
    That child or man, who will or can
    Be merry on my day,
    To bliss thou bring – and I shall sing,
    Lullay, by, by, lullay.'

Anon. 15th Century. Bodleian MS. Eng. Poet. e.l. and Balliol MS. 354
The 'Oxford Book of Carols' says: 'It was not new when it was written out in
the Bodleian MS. dated between 1460 and 1490.

[1] The other night.   [2] *ever among* = every now and then.   [3] *veray* = true.   [4] *light* = alight.
[5] *no nay* = not to be denied.   [6] *pay* = satisfaction.   [7] *in fay* = in faith.   [8] *skill* = Reasonable.

175   MY DANCING DAY
(UNACC.)

English Traditional
Arranged, E. P.

Lightly, with a dance pulse (one-in-a-bar stress) ♩. = 66

SOLO or GROUP

1 To-morrow shall be— my danc-ing day: I would my
2 Then was— I born of a vir-gin pure, Of her— I
3 In a man-ger laid— and wrapped I was, So ve-ry

true— love did— so chance   To— see the le-gend
took— flesh-ly— sub-stànce;   Thus was I knit to
poor, this was— my chance,   Be-twixt an ox and a

175 (continued)

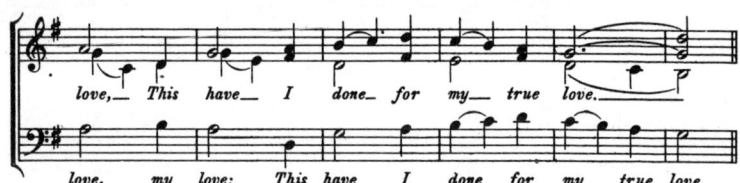

love,— This have— I done— for my— true love.———
love, my love; This have I done for my— true love.

Either refrain, or both, may be used, in optional order
© Elizabeth Poston

1 Tomorrow shall be my dancing day:
  I would my true love did so chance
  To see the legend of my play,
  To call my true love to my dance:
   Sing O my love, O my love, my love, my love;
   This have I done for my true love.

2 Then was I born of a virgin pure,
  Of her I took fleshly substance;
  Thus was I knit to man's nature;
  To call my true love to my dance:

3 In a manger laid and wrapped I was,
  So very poor, this was my chance,
  Betwixt an ox and a silly poor ass,
  To call my true love to my dance:

English traditional, from Sandys, 1833

176 MY DANCING DAY
(ACC.)

Lightly, with a dance pulse
(one-in-a-bar stress) ♩.= 66

English traditional melody, from W. Sandys,
Christmas Carols Ancient and Modern, 1833
Arranged, E. P.

Verses 1, 2, 3 Solo or Unison group
Verse 4 4-Part or Unison

To-morrow shall be my danc-ing day: I would my true love did so chance To see the le-gend of my play, To call my true love to my dance:

REFRAIN: Tutti

© Elizabeth Poston

177 WHAT TIDINGS BRING'ST US, MESSENGER?

15th-century carol tune, Trinity College, Cambridge, MS. o.3.58
Arranged Elizabeth Poston, 1905–

BURDEN
Joyous and flowing

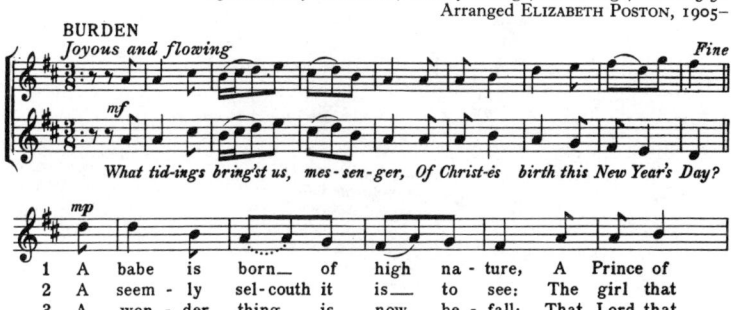

What tid-ings bring'st us, mes-sen-ger, Of Christ-ès birth this New Year's Day?

1 A babe is born of high na-ture, A Prince of Peace that ev-er shall be; Of heav'n and earth he hath the cure, His lord-ship is e-ter-ni-ty. Such won-der tid-ings ye may hear: That God and man are
2 A seem-ly sel-couth it is to see: The girl that hath this bairn y-borne, This child con-ceived in high de-gree, And maid-en is as was be-forne. Such won-der tid-ings ye may hear: That maid-en and mo-ther is
3 A won-der thing is now be-fall: That Lord that made both sea and sun, Heav'n and earth and an-gels all, In man-kind is now be-come. What tid-ings bring'st us, mes-sen-ger? A child that is but
4 This love-ly la-dy did greet her child: 'Hail son, hail bro-ther, hail fa-ther dear!' 'Hail daugh-ter, hail sis-ter, hail mo-ther mild!' This hail-ing was in wise man-ner. Such won-der tid-ings ye may hear: This greet-ing was of
5 That Lord that all things made of naught Is man be-come for man's love, For with his blood he shall be bought From bale to bliss that is a-bove. Such won-der tid-ings ye may now hear: That Lord us grant

177 (continued)

brought	more near,	Our	sin had	made	us	fiend - ès	prey.
one—	crea - ture	And	la - dy	is	of	high ar -	ray.
of—	one year	Ev -	er has	been	and	shall be	aye.
so—	high cheer	That	man's	pain	it	turned to	play.
now—	our prayer,	To	dwell in	heav -	en	that— we	may.

What tidings bring'st us, messenger,
Of Christès birth this New Year's Day.[1]

1 A babe is born of high nature,
   A Prince of Peace that ever shall be;
Of heaven and earth he hath the cure,[1]
   His lordship is eternity.
     Such wonder tidings ye may hear:
     That God and man are brought more near,
     Our sin had made us fiendès prey.

2 A seemly selcouth[2] it is to see:
   The girl that hath this bairn yborne,
This child conceived in high degree,
   And maiden is as was beforne.
     Such wonder tidings ye may hear:
     That maiden and mother is one creature
     And lady is of high array.

3 A wonder thing is now befall:
   That Lord that made both sea and sun,
Heaven and earth and angels all,
   In mankind is now become.
     What tidings bring'st us, messenger?
     A child that is but of one year
     Ever has been and shall be aye.

4 This lovely lady did greet her child:
   'Hail son, hail brother, hail father dear!'
'Hail daughter, hail sister, hail mother mild!'
   This hailing was in wise manner.
     Such wonder tidings ye may hear:
     This greeting was of so high cheer
     That man's pain it turned to play.

5 That Lord that all things made of naught
   Is man become for man's love,
For with his blood he shall be bought
   From bale to bliss that is above.
     Such wonder tidings ye may now hear:
     That Lord us grant now our prayer,
     To dwell in heaven that we may.

Burden and stanzas 1, 2, 3, 4: Trinity College, Cambridge, MS. 0.3.58
     15th century. By John Audelay (?)
     stanza 5: Bodleian Library MS.

---

[1] *cure* = spiritual charge, also the capacity to heal.
[2] *seemly selcouth* = marvellous ('seldom known') thing.

178

WINCHESTER OLD Este's *Psalter*, 1592

Melody in the Tenor T. RAVENSCROFT in his *Psalter*, 1621
UNISON

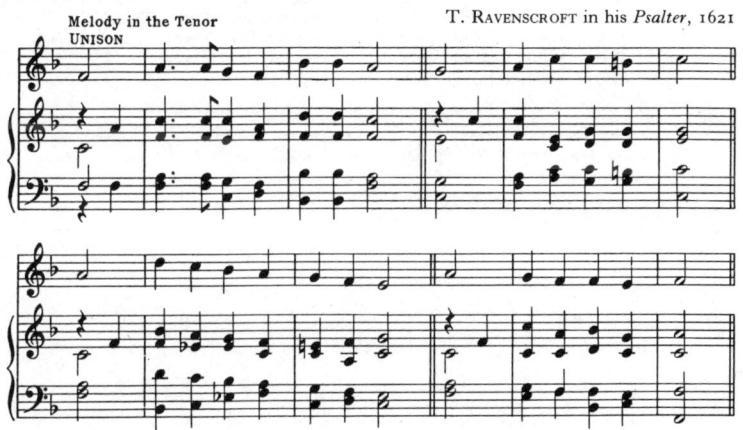

1 While shepherds watched their flocks by night,
  All seated on the ground,
 The angel of the Lord came down,
  And glory shone around.

2 'Fear not,' said he (for mighty dread
  Had seized their troubled mind);
 'Glad tidings of great joy I bring
  To you and all mankind.

3 'To you in David's town this day
  Is born of David's line
 A Saviour, who is Christ the Lord;
  And this shall be the sign:

4 'The heavenly babe you there shall find
  To human view displayed,
 All meanly wrapped in swathing[1] bands
  And in a manger laid.'

5 Thus spake the seraph; and forthwith
  Appeared a shining throng
 Of angels praising God, who thus
  Addressed their joyful song:

6 'All glory be to God on high,
  And to the earth be peace;
 Goodwill henceforth from heaven to men
  Begin and never cease.'

Nahum Tate, 1652–1715

[1] Pronounce 'swaything.'

179 A NEW YEAR CAROL

BENJAMIN BRITTEN, 1913–

Copyright 1936 by Boosey & Co. Ltd.
Reprinted by permission of Boosey & Hawkes Music Publishers Ltd.

1 Here we bring new water from the well so clear,
  For to worship God with, this happy New Year.
  Sing levy dew, sing levy dew, the water and the wine;
  The seven bright gold wires and the bugles that do shine.

2 Sing reign of Fair Maid, with gold upon her toe,
  Open you the West Door, and turn the Old Year go.

3 Sing reign of Fair Maid, with gold upon her chin,
  Open you the East Door, and let the New Year in.

Traditional

TWELFTH NIGHT SONG
TWO-PART UNACC. WITH A
CONCLUDING ROUND FOR 4 VOICES

ELIZABETH MACONCHY, 1907–
Commissioned for *The Cambridge Hymnal*

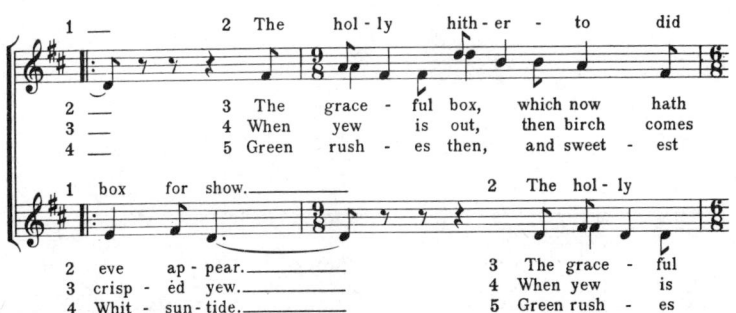

180 (continued)

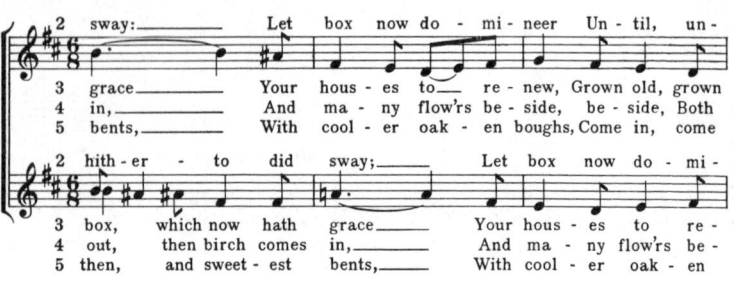

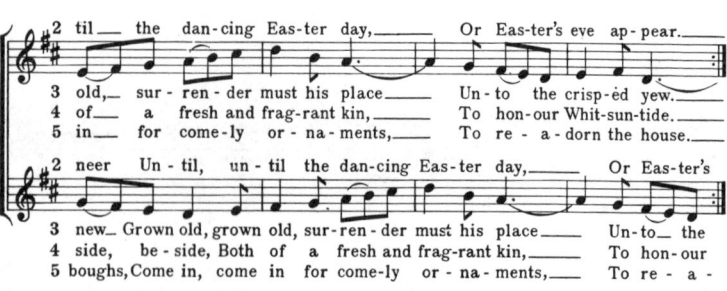

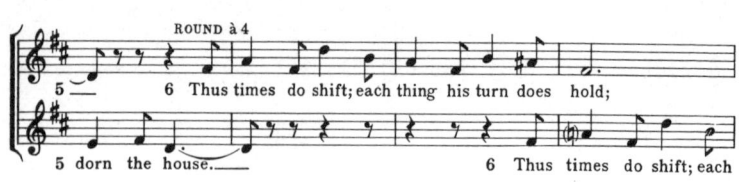

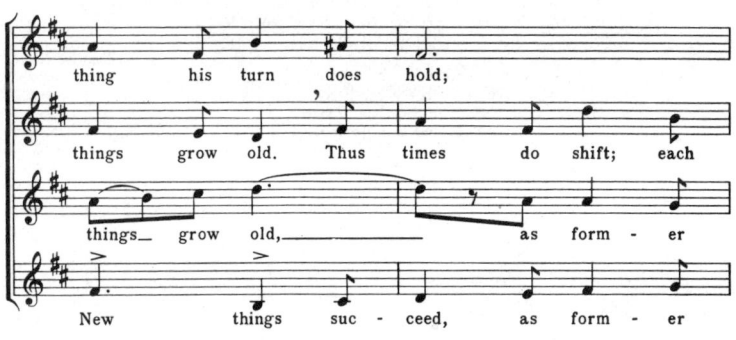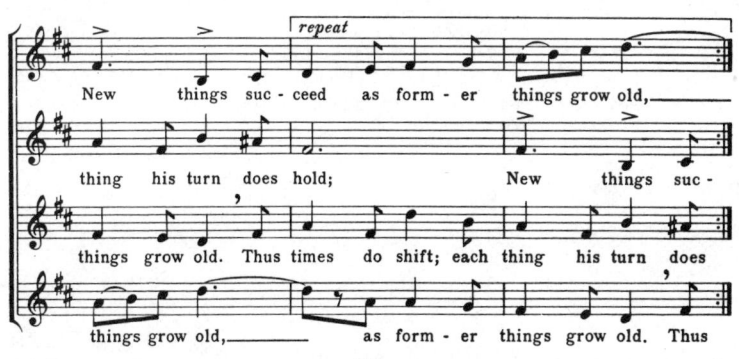

180 (continued)

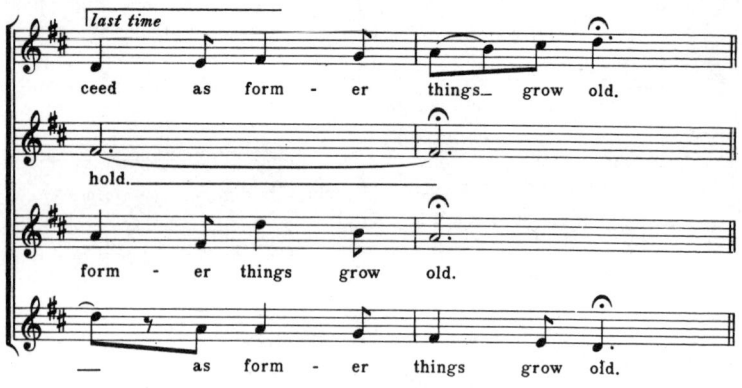

1. Down with the rosemary and bays,
   Down with the mistletoe;
   Instead of holly, now upraise
   The greener box, for show.

2. The holly hitherto did sway:
   Let box now domineer
   Until the dancing Easter day,
   Or Easter's eve appear.

3. The graceful box, which now hath grace
   Your houses to renew,
   Grown old, surrender must his place
   Unto the crispèd yew.

4. When yew is out, then birch comes in,
   And many flowers beside,
   Both of a fresh and fragrant kin,
   To honour Whitsuntide.

5. Green rushes then, and sweetest bents,
   With cooler oaken boughs,
   Come in for comely ornaments,
   To re-adorn the house.

6. Thus times do shift; each thing his turn does hold;
   New things succeed, as former things grow old.

Robert Herrick, 1591-1674

APPENDIX

181 ALLELUIA
CANON 9 IN 1

JOHN GARDNER, 1917–
Commissioned for *The Cambridge Hymnal*

182 ALLELUIA

A. T. OLA-OLUDE, from the Yoruba, *Ora Elese T'oku*.
Arranged FELA SOWANDE
Commissioned for *The Cambridge Hymnal*

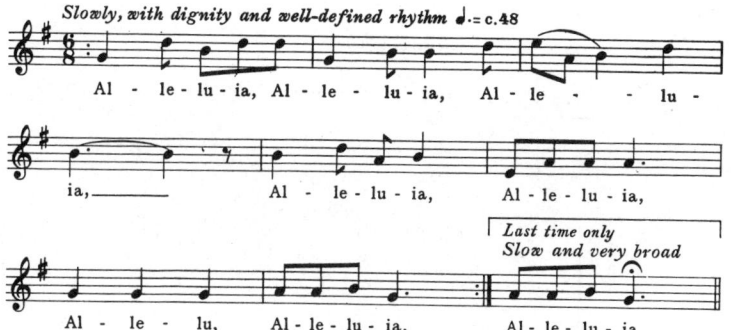

May be sung cumulatively/antiphonally, adding voices or groups of voices.

ALLELUIA

IGOR STRAVINSKY, 1882–1971
Adapted, E. P.

If sung accompanied, it may be found preferable for Voice 3 to enter at the sixth bar.
Printed by permission of J. & W. Chester Ltd.

184   ALLELUIA FOR HIGH VOICES
ON A PLAINSONG MELODY

Guy Oldham, 1929–
Arrangement commissioned and adapted for *The Cambridge Hymnal*

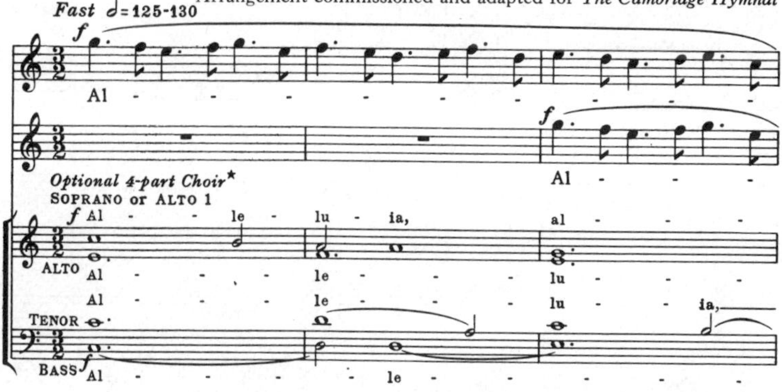

* May sing to 'ah' if preferred.
  May be sung twice through, first time f, second time p, or vice versa, as preferred.

185

TONUS PEREGRINUS

Plainsong setting by J. S. BACH, 1685–1750
Cantata No. 10

Glory be to God the Father, and the Son, and to the Holy Ghost: as it was in the beginning, is now, and for ever shall be, world without end. Amen.

THE QUEEN'S HYMN

ELIZABETH POSTON 1905–

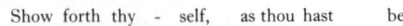

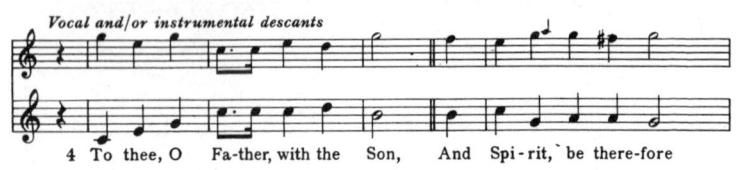

1 Lord, keep Elizabeth our Queen,
  Defend her in thy right:
 Show forth thyself, as thou hast been,
  Her fortress and her might.

2 Her Counsel, Lord, vouchsafe to guide,
  With wisdom let them shine,
 In godliness for to abide,
  As it becometh thine.

3 So will we sing unto thee, Lord,
  Betime, ere day be light;
 And so declare thy truth abroad
  When it doth draw to night.

4 To thee, O Father, with the Son,
  And Spirit, be therefore
 All glory now, as hath been done,
  From henceforth evermore.

From the Accession Service of Queen Elizabeth I, 1558

ROUNDS AND CANONS

187 AMEN
(CANON 9 IN 1)

JOHN GARDNER, 1917–

188 AS THE TREE FALLS
(CANON 4 IN 1)

JOHN GARDNER, 1917–
Commissioned for *The Cambridge Hymnal*

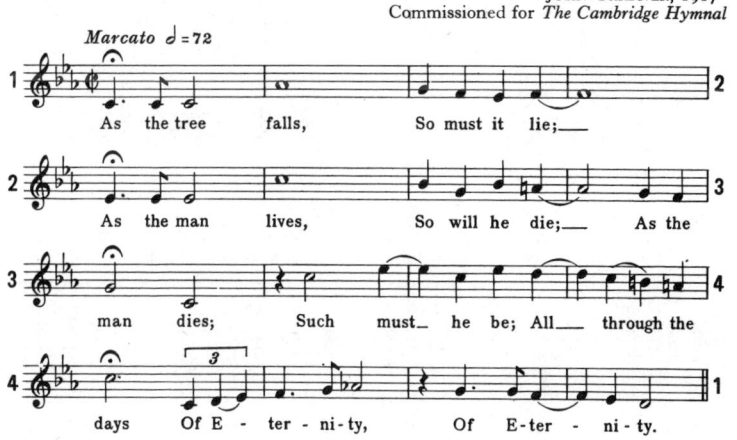

As the tree falls,
  So must it lie;
As the man lives,
  So will he die;
As the man dies,
  Such must he be;
All through the days
  Of Eternity.

E. Caswall (1814–1878). *From 'The Masque of Mary'* (1858)

NON NOBIS, DOMINE
3-PART CANON

Attributed to WILLIAM BYRD, 1543–1623

Non nobis, Domine, non nobis, sed nomini tuo da gloriam.
Not unto us, O Lord, not unto us, but unto thy name be the praise.
Psalm CXV

190 ROUND

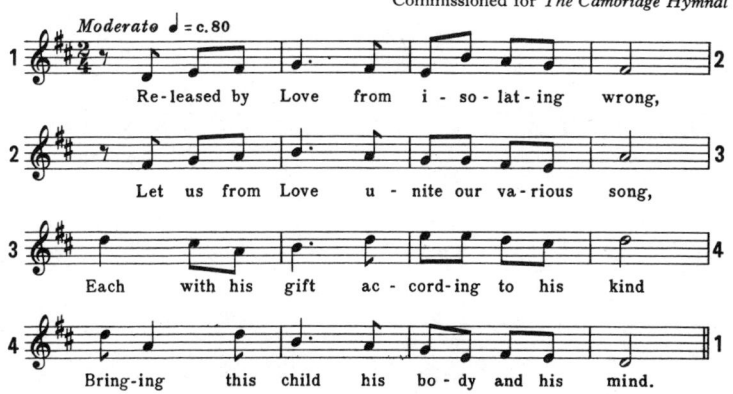

Released by Love from isolating wrong,
Let us from Love unite our various song,
Each with his gift according to his kind
Bringing this child his body and his mind.

W. H. Auden, 1907–1973
(In 'A Christmas Oratorio'). From 'For the Time Being,' 1947

191 ACCOMPANIED CANON FOR TWO VOICES

191 (continued)

192

SUMMA
(A ROUND)

WILLIAM WORDSWORTH, 1908–
Commissioned for *The Cambridge Hymnal*

The best ideal is the true
And other truth is none.
All glory be ascribèd to
The holy Three in One.

Gerard Manley Hopkins, 1844–89

193 ROUND

ELIZABETH POSTON, 1905–

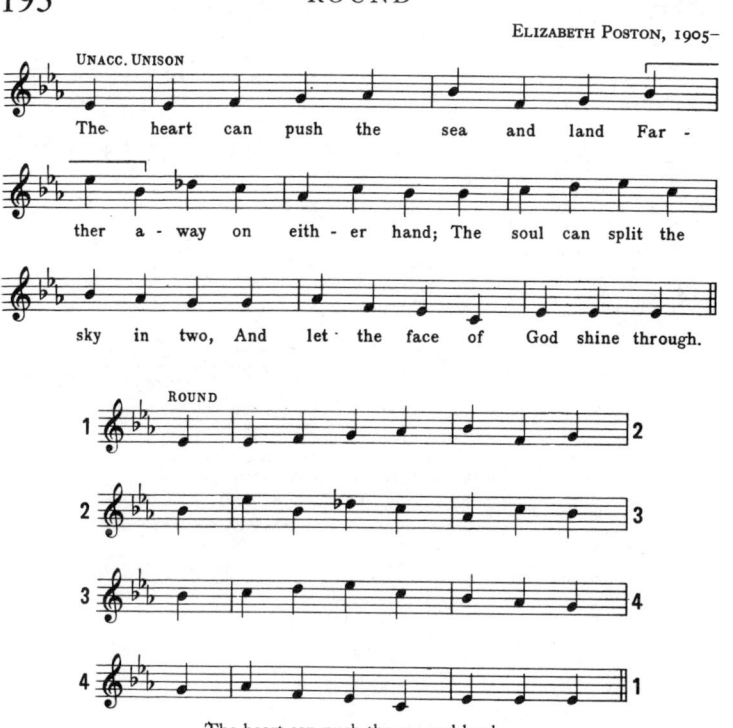

The heart can push the sea and land
Farther away on either hand;
The soul can split the sky in two,
And let the face of God shine through.

Edna St. Vincent Millay, 1892–1950

From 'Renascence' in Renascence and other poems, Harper Brothers
Copyright, 1912, by Edna St. Vincent Millay

194

WILLIAM BILLINGS, 1746-1800
In 'The New England Psalm Singer,' 1770

When Jesus wept, the falling tear
In mercy flowed beyond all bound;
When Jesus groaned, a trembling fear
Seized all the guilty world around.

'The New England Psalm Singer,' 1770

INDEX

Roman type is used for first lines; italics for titles; the third column gives tunes

A babe is born of high nature	177	—
A virgin most pure, as the prophets do tell	141	—
Accompanied Canon for two voices	191	—
Adam lay ybounden	140	—
Adeste fideles	164	Adeste Fideles
Ah, holy Jesu, how hast thou offended	2	Herzliebster Jesu
Ah! my dear Lord! what couldst thou spy	1	Gynack
All glory, laud and honour	3	St Theodulph; St Theodulph (Valet will ich dir geben)
All people that on earth do dwell	4	Old Hundredth
All this night shrill chanticleer	142	—
Alleluia	181, 182, 183	—
Alleluia! Alleluia! Alleluia!	86	O Filii et Filiae
Alleluia for high voices	184, 185	—
Amen	187	—
And now another day is gone	5	Song 47
Antiphon	58	St Teilo
As pants the hart for cooling streams	6	Martyrdom
As the tree falls	188	—
Balulalow	163	—
Be with me, Lord, where'er I go	7	Wareham
Before the ending of the day	8	Compline Hymn; Te Lucis ante Terminum
Before the ending of the day	105	Te Lucis; St Ambrose (plainchant)
Behold a silly tender babe	143	—
Blest are the pure in heart	9	Franconia
Blest be the day that I began	10	Tiverton
Boar's Head Carol, The	144	—
Bread of the world in mercy broken	11	Rendez à Dieu
Call, The	21	The Call
Can I see another's woe	12	Tunbridge
Cast thy burden upon the Lord	13	Cast thy Burden
Chanticleer's Carol	142	—
Charity	83	—
Christ was the Word who spake it	22	Nun lasst uns Gott
Christ, whose glory fills the skies	15	Ratisbon
Christmas Day	159	—
Come, Holy Ghost, our souls inspire	121	Veni Creator (plainchant)
Come, Holy Ghost, our souls inspire	123	Jam Lucis (plainchant)
Come, Holy Ghost, our souls inspire	126	Veni Creator
Come, Holy Ghost, thine influence shed	14	Walsall
Come, Holy Ghost, who ever one	17	Babylon's streams
Come, Holy Ghost, who ever one	122	Babylon's streams
Come, let us join our cheerful songs	19	Nativity
Come, my soul, thy suit prepare	20	Song 13
Come, my way, my truth, my life	21	The Call
Come, O come in pious lays	22	St George (2)
Corpus Christi Carol	145	—
Coverdale's Carol	170	—
Creator Spirit, by whose aid	125	Colchester
Dead upon the tree, my Saviour	24	Judicium
Death and darkness get you packing	25	—
Deo Gratias	140	—
Discipline	115	The Gentle Path
Down in yon forest there stands a hall	145	—
Down with the rosemary and bays	180	—
Enrich, Lord, heart, mouth, hands in me	27	Geneva; 36 (First strain)
Eternal Father, strong to save	26	Melita
Eternal God, we look to thee	28	Tallis's Ordinal ('9th Tune')
Eternal Power, whose high abode	29	Uffingham
Evening Hymn	77	—

189

Experience does me so inspire	30	Dunbar
Fisherman Peter on the sea	32	—
For Saturday	76	
Forth in thy name, O Lord, I go	31	Angel's Song
Francis Kindlemarsh's Carol	147	—
From virgin's womb this Christmas day did spring	147	Song 24
Glory be to God the Father	185	Tonus Peregrinus
Glory to thee, my God, this night	33	Tallis's Canon
God be in my head	36	Morlich
God moves in a mysterious way	37	London New
God of the morning, at whose voice	38	Truro
God rest you merry, Gentlemen	148	—
Godhead here in hiding whom I do adore	35	Adoro Te
Hail the day that sees him rise	39	Llanfair
Hark, the herald angels sing	149	Mendelssohn
He is the Way	41	Santa Barbara
He shall the broken heart repair	43	Lutton
He that is down needs fear no fall	44	Plumstead
He wants not friends that hath thy love	42	Yellow Bittern
Hear'st thou, my soul, what serious things	40	Boar's Hill
Herbert's Twenty-third Psalme	101	Bicclescombe
Here we bring new water from the well so clear	179	—
How happy is he born and taught	45	Solothurn
How lovely are thy dwellings fair	46	Durham
How shall I sing that majesty	48	Old 22nd
Hush! my dear, lie still and slumber	151	—
Hymn to God the Father, A	130	—
I call on the Lord Jesu Christ	49	Steadfast
I saw a fair maiden	161	—
I sing of a maiden	152	—
I sing the birth was born tonight	157	Whitland
If God build not the house	50	Vater Unser
In a field as I lay	153	—
In Bethlehem in that fair city	162	—
In the bleak mid-winter	154	Cranham
In this world (the Isle of Dreams)	51	Brookend
Into this world this day did come	156	—
It was poor little Jesus	155	—
Jesus born in Beth'ny	158	—
Jesus Christ is risen today	53	Easter Hymn
Jesus Christ the Apple Tree	111	—
Jesus, Lord, that madest me	52	Prayer
Jesus shall reign where'er the sun	54	Galilee
King of glory, King of peace	55	Gwalchmai
King of mercy, King of love	56	Halton Holgate
Last night in the open shippen	159	—
Let all the world in ev'ry corner sing	58	St Teilo
Let saints on earth in concert sing	57	Dundee (Faux-bourdon)
Let us with a gladsome mind	59	Monkland
Lift up to heav'n, sad wretch, thy heavy sprite	60	Peerson
Lord, by whose breath all souls and seeds are living	61	Wiveton
Lord, dismiss us with thy blessing	63	Compton Scorpion
Lord, I have made thy work my choice	64	Wetherby
Lord, in the strength of grace	65	Song 20
Lord, it belongs not to my care	66	Ashwell
Lord Jesus, think on me	67	Southwell
Lord, keep Elizabeth our Queen	186	—
Lord of our life, and God of our salvation	68	Iste Confessor
Lord, when the wise men came from far	69	St Venantius
Love divine, all loves excelling	70	Hyfrydol
Love's redeeming work is done	71	Jouissance
Lullay, lullay, thou lytil child	160	—
Lullay my liking	161	—
May the grace of Christ our Saviour	74	Gott des Himmels
Most glorious Lord of life, that on this day	72	Farley Castle
My Dancing Day	175, 176	—
My Shepherd will supply my need	102	Glen
My soul, there is a country	73	Christus der ist mein Leben

Never weather-beaten sail more willing bent to shore	75	—
New Year Carol, A	179	—
Non nobis, Domine	189	—
Now that the sun has veiled his light	77	—
Nowell, Nowell, Nowell	162	Burden
Now's the time for mirth and play	76	—
O come, all ye faithful	164	Adeste Fideles
O come, let us sing to the Lord	78	Bon Accord
O God, my strength and fortitude	81	Song 67
O most merciful	82	Schönster Herr Jesu
O my deir heart, young Jesus sweet	163	—
O Queen of virtues, whose sweet pow'r	83	—
O sacred head, sore wounded	84	Passion Chorale
O sons and daughters let us sing	86	O Filii et Filiae
O worship the King, all glorious above	85	Hanover
On Christmas night all Christians sing	165	—
Our Church Palms are budding Willow Twigs	131	—
Our God, our help in ages past	79	St Anne; Faux-bourdon
Pleasure it is	88	—
Poor little Jesus	155	—
Praise, my soul, the King of heaven	87	Praise, my soul
Praise to the Holiest in the height	89	Elgar
Pray that Jerusalem may have	90	York; Faux-bourdon
Queen's Hymn, The	186	—
Qui creavit coelum	166	—
Rejoice! the Lord is King	91	Gopsal
Released by love from isolating wrong	190	—
Richard de Castre's Prayer to Jesus	52	Prayer
Round	193	—
Simple Gifts	117	—
Sing a song of joy	92	—
Sing, all men! 'tis Christmas morning	167	—
Soldiers of Christ, arise	94	St Ethelwald
Sometimes a light surprises	93	Offertorium
Suddenly afraid, half-waking, half-sleeping	95	—
Summa	192	—
Sweet day, so cool, so calm, so bright	96	PenSelwood
Sweet Infancy	97	Feshie
Sweet was the song the Virgin sung	168	—
Te lucis ante terminum	8	Compline Hymn; Te Lucis ante Terminun
Te lucis ante terminum	105	Te Lucis; St Ambrose
Teach me, my God and King	104	Sandys
That Lord that lay in assé stall	169	—
That virgin's child	106	—
The best ideal is the true	192	—
The blessed son of God only	170	—
The boar's head in hand bear I	144	—
The first Nowell the Angel did say	146	—
The God of Abraham praise	107	Leoni
The God of love my Shepherd is	99	University
The God of love my Shepherd is	101	Bicclescombe
The head that once was crowned with thorns	112	St Magnus (Nottingham)
The heart can push the sea and land	193	—
The holly and the ivy	150	—
The holy Son of God most high	148	Jena (Das neugeborne Kindelein)
The Lord my pasture shall prepare	100	Surrey
The Lord of Heav'n confess	138	Darwall's 148th
The Lord, the Lord my Shepherd is	98	Speyside
The Lord will come, and be not slow	109	Old 107th
The Lord's my Shepherd, I'll not want	103	Crimond
The night is come, like to the day	110	Oakley
The spacious firmament on high	34	Tallis's Canon
The tree of life my soul hath seen	111	—
The virgin Mary had a baby boy	171	—
The water stood like walls of brass	113	St Olaf's
There is no rose of such virtue	172, 173	—

This endris night	174	—
Thou art my life; if thou but turn away	114	Löwenstern (Heut' ist O Mensch); Hymn Tune Prelude
Thou wast, O God, and thou wast blest	116	Third Mode Melody; Melody in the Tenor
Throw away thy rod	115	The Gentle Path
Thy mercy, Lord, is in the heavens	37	London New
'Tis the gift to be simple, 'tis the gift to be free	117	—
To Mercy, Pity, Peace, and Love	118	Bishops
Tomorrow shall be my dancing day	175, 176	—
Twelfth Night Carol	162	—
Twelfth Night Song	180	—
Up to those bright and gladsome hills	119	Newcastle
Veni, Creator Spiritus	120	Veni Creator (plainchant)
View me, Lord, a work of thine	127	—
Watts's Cradle Song	151	—
Were you there when they crucified my Lord	132	Refrain
What creature, O sweet Lord	133	Old 25th
What tidings bring'st us, messenger?	177	—
What wondrous love is this, O my soul	135	Wondrous Love
What's this that in my soul is rising	134	Mercy's Free
When all thy mercies, O my God	136	Belgrave
When Jesus wept, the falling tear	194	—
Where Riches is Everlastingly	156	—
While Christ lay dead the widowed world	131	Pastheen
While shepherds watched their flocks by night	178	Winchester old
Who would true valour see	128	Monks Gate
Wilt thou forgive that sin, where I began	130	Donne
Wise men patience never want	129	—
With all the powers my poor soul hath	137	Rockingham
Ye holy angels bright	138	Darwall's 148th
You that have spent the silent night	139	Gräfenberg